# TABLE OF CONTENTS

Receive Power .................................................................. 5

How Do I Receive the Power ...................................... 13

Power Over Insecurity ................................................... 30

Power Over Anxiety ....................................................... 38

Power Over Depression ................................................ 45

Power Over Addiction ................................................... 54

Power Over Suffering .................................................... 65

Power Over Anger .......................................................... 77

Power In Relationships ................................................. 85

Power Over Bitterness ................................................ 108

Power At Your Job ....................................................... 123

Power In Your Finances ............................................. 129

Power to Persevere ...................................................... 139

Summary ....................................................................... 145

References ..................................................................... 149

Thank You for picking up this book. The Biblical principles within these pages can transform your life! Each chapter covers a different aspect of your relationship with self, others, and God. Even chapters that do not relate directly to your situation may help and encourage you. For example: You may not struggle with bitterness but it can still hurt when people do or say offensive things to you. The Power Over Bitterness chapter provides Biblical wisdom to help address those hurts. Guidelines presented in a chapter unrelated to you may be just what you need in another area of your life. At the very least, I urge you to read the first and last chapters (Receive Power and Power to Persevere).

This book is designed to help change your thoughts and actions. You can't change others but you can change yourself. In the process, others are more likely to change in a positive way. Focus on personal growth and watch how God improves both yourself and your surroundings.

May God be with you as you pursue a healthier and happier life...

*Now the God of hope fill you with all joy and peace in believing, that ye may abound in hope, through the power of the Holy Ghost.*
                              Romans 15:13

# Receive Power
By Brett A Saburn
First Edition, 2022

Unless otherwise noted, Bible quotes are from the original King James Version

Scripture quotations marked (CEV) are from the Contemporary English Version Copyright © 1991, 1992, 1995 by American Bible Society, Used by Permission

Cover and artwork by Heather Reece
https://heathermariedesigns.com/

Copyright © 2022 Brett Saburn

All rights reserved

 Brett Saburn is an Administrative Pastor at the Refuge of Hope church in Andover, Minnesota, where he has been a member for over 30 years

# Receive Power

When my brother Keith was two weeks old he needed emergency bypass surgery to replace a malformed artery. The resulting scar tissue necessitated an additional bypass at the age of twelve. In both situations, a highly skilled surgeon performed an amazingly delicate operation that we practically take for granted nowadays. After the 2nd surgery, everything seemed fine until a few days later, when we rushed him back to the hospital. Today my brother is the survivor of multiple strokes, resulting from a mistake made during the operation. He only has the use of one arm, walks with a gait, and struggles communicating.

It's simply a matter of time. No matter how independent and capable you may be, sooner or later life will hit you with something that you cannot control. A healthy diet and exercise does not guarantee a life without health issues. Wealth cannot buy a strong relationship with your children. Wisdom and caution may not prevent a tragic accident. Enjoying addictive substances in moderation does not mean you will not become addicted. Popularity does not prevent loneliness and depression. A life filled with self-gratification does not protect you from feeling empty and unfulfilled. The list goes on and on. Sooner or later life will leave you feeling powerless. Maybe you are in that state right now.

Amazingly talented people saved my brother's life, and I am grateful for them, but people have limitations and make mistakes. In this case, they can replace an artery, but they can't make his arm work again. They can help his speech impediments with therapy, but they can't fix the brain damage that makes it hard to put thoughts into words. They can fit him with a prosthetic arm to replace his hand, but they can't make a process like tying ones shoes simple again. They can teach him new life skills, but they can't help much when his best friend alienates him as a result of his new handicap.

Billions of dollars are spent each year on counselors, psychologists, psychiatrists, physicians, and other experts as people seek a way through their situations. Some turn to hedonism, yoga, philanthropy, support groups, and other strategies to redirect their mindset. Sadly, some turn to illegal drugs, alcohol, and even suicide as they try to drown out the pain in their lives.

It's important and needful to build positive relationships with people on both a personal and professional level. We need others for support, guidance, help and encouragement, but humans are limited in their ability and may even hurt you further. The relationship you need most is with God! He knows everything and has the power to do anything. He knows you better than you even know yourself and He wants to help you…

*The thief cometh not, but for to steal, and to kill, and to destroy: I [Jesus] am come that they might have life, and <u>that they might have it more abundantly</u>.* – John 10:10

However, there are two important things that you need to know…
1. God will not force himself upon you. You need to seek a relationship with Him
2. God is perfect and will not have a relationship with someone that is not pursuing improvement in their life

Obviously perfection is an impossibility. We all have a past and will all make unwise choices in our future. These wrong thoughts, attitudes and actions are referred to as sin, making us unfit to be in God's presence. But there is great news! God loves us so much that He took on humanity and became a man for the sole purpose of covering our sin and restoring the opportunity for a relationship with Him. This human being that was God himself is referred to as the Son in the Bible and His name is Jesus…

RECEIVE POWER

*For God so loved the world, that he gave his only begotten Son, that whosoever believeth in him should not perish, but have everlasting life.* – John 3:16

*But as many as <u>received him</u> [Jesus Christ], to them gave he <u>power to become the sons of God</u> [relationship], even to them that <u>believe on his name</u>* - John 1:12

So the first question we need to ask ourselves is 'How do I start a relationship with God and receive the power that He has for me?.' Jesus himself points us towards the answer to this question and then the Apostle Peter provides the details. Before Jesus left this earth he explained…

*…it behoved Christ [Jesus] to <u>suffer</u>, and to <u>rise from the dead</u> the third day: 47 And that <u>repentance and remission of sins</u> should be preached in his name among all nations, <u>beginning at Jerusalem</u>.* – Luke 24:46-47

As mentioned earlier, Jesus paid the penalty for our sin by dying for us. This was an excruciating death by Roman crucifixion. However, Jesus defeated death by coming to life again, just as the Bible predicted. Because of this, forgiveness of our sins is made available to us so we can have a relationship with God. This 'New Testament' was to begin at Jerusalem. He then went on to say…

*…tarry ye in the city of Jerusalem, until ye be endued with power from on high.* – Luke 24:49

Shortly after making these statements Jesus ascended up into heaven. Those that heard Him speak these words returned to Jerusalem and tarried as instructed. Seven days[17] later we read where the power was given…

*And when the day of Pentecost was fully come, they were all with one accord in one place. 2 And suddenly there came a sound from heaven as of a rushing mighty wind, and it filled all the house where they were sitting. 3 And there appeared unto them cloven tongues like as of fire, and it sat upon each of them. 4 And <u>they were all filled with the Holy Ghost</u>, and began to speak with other tongues, as the Spirit gave them utterance.* – Acts 2:1-4

They received power from God via the infilling of the Holy Ghost. Luke, the author of the book of Acts, confirms this connection in Acts chapter 1, before he even begins telling the story in chapter 2, by quoting Jesus himself…

*ye shall receive power, <u>after that the Holy Ghost is come upon you</u>…* - Acts 1:8

The commotion that ensued attracted the attention of a lot of bystanders who wanted to know what was going on. The Apostle Peter proceeded to explain to them that this was God pouring out His spirit upon them as promised in the Bible…

RECEIVE POWER

*But this is that which was spoken by the prophet Joel; 17 And it shall come to pass in the last days, saith God, I will pour out of my Spirit upon all flesh:* - Acts 2:16-17

He then went on to explain that they were sinners before God, in this case because they specifically took part in the death of Jesus Christ. When the people heard Peter's message, they were convicted in their hearts and wanted to make amends...

*Now when they heard this, they were pricked in their heart, and said unto Peter and to the rest of the apostles, Men and brethren, what shall we do?* – Acts 2:37

Peter then shared how we are to address the wrong doings (sin) in our lives, how to restore our relationship with God, and how to receive the power of the Holy Ghost...

*Then Peter said unto them, <u>Repent</u>, and <u>be baptized</u> every one of you <u>in the name of Jesus Christ</u> for the remission of sins, <u>and ye shall receive the gift of the Holy Ghost</u>.* – Acts 2:38

Over 3000 people turned their hearts to God that day and this same promise is for us today!

*For the promise is unto you, and to your children, and to all that are afar off, even as many as the Lord our God shall call. 40 And with many other words did he testify and exhort, saying, Save yourselves from this untoward generation.-* Acts 2:39-40

Just as Peter encouraged everyone who heard his voice that day to turn to God, I encourage you to pursue a relationship with Him today! You will find nothing on this earth that can fulfil you like the power and presence of the Holy Ghost! Humanity is in a never ending quest to find contentment, peace and happiness in their lives. At best it is merely temporary and fleeting without God. Turn to Him today!

Countless times over the years I've heard Christians mocked as people who need a 'crutch' in their lives in order to survive, because we are too weak to handle reality on our own. That we live and stand upon a false hope that some make believe God is out there to help us. I can tell you without a doubt, that anyone who has ever experienced the power of God in their lives by receiving the Holy Ghost, knows that He is absolutely real and powerful. There may be some who would deny God and His power to your face but deep down inside they know better. If they don't, they never received it to begin with.

To feel that you are exhibiting weakness by turning to God is both correct and crazy…
- We are weak: To think that we can handle anything that comes our way in life is simply a lie. The proof is in society's rampant issues with

suicide, addictions, overflowing prisons, drugs, etc. Everyone turns to something…some are just more obvious than others.
- It's crazy to feel that turning to God is exhibiting weakness: Anyone who is serious about anything gets the best help they can. Sports enthusiasts hire personal coaches. Politicians pay for opinion polls and consultants. People serious about their career pursue ongoing education and mentorship. The list goes on and on and yet nobody feels weak or foolish in these pursuits. They understand that these are key elements to growth and success. Why would you feel any differently about God?

The Bible tells us…

*the fruit of the Spirit* [Holy Ghost] *is love, joy, peace, longsuffering, gentleness, goodness, faith, Meekness, temperance: against such there is no law.* – Galatians 5:22-23

*Therefore if any man be in Christ, he is a new creature: old things are passed away; behold, <u>all things are become new</u>.* – 2 Corinthians 5:17

This sounds more like wisdom than weakness. Are you ready to trade in hatred for love? Anger for gentleness? Despair for faith? Impatience for longsuffering? Give yourself to God today and receive the power that will transform your life!

# How Do I Receive the Power

In the previous chapter, we learned that in order to receive the power of God in our lives, we need to repent, be baptized, and receive the Holy Ghost as explained by the Apostle Peter…

*Then Peter said unto them, Repent, and be baptized every one of you in the name of Jesus Christ for the remission of sins, and ye shall receive the gift of the Holy Ghost.* – Acts 2:38

Obviously, one short statement can leave as many questions as it does answers. For one thing, what about other verses that talk about receiving power, or being saved, or having eternal life? We quoted two such verses in the last chapter…

*For God so loved the world, that he gave his only begotten Son, that <u>whosoever believeth in him</u> should not perish, but have everlasting life.* – John 3:16

*But as many as <u>received him</u> [Jesus Christ], to them gave he power to become the sons of God [relationship], even to them that <u>believe on his name</u>* - John 1:12

These two verses imply that you only need to

believe in and receive Jesus. Does the Bible contradict itself, giving various methods to receive the same results? To properly understand the Bible, you need to combine it as a whole. You cannot just take one verse and create a belief system from it. It must mesh with the rest of the Bible.

We best understand Acts 2:38 when we realize that approximately seven[17] days prior, Jesus promised to send the power, that it would be tied to remission of sins, and that it would start in Jerusalem (as noted in the previous chapter - Luke 24:46-49). One scripture that we have not covered up to this point further confirms that Acts 2:38 is a key verse. Jesus said…

*…thou art <u>Peter</u>, and upon this rock I will build my church; and the gates of hell shall not prevail against it. 19 And I will give unto thee <u>the keys of the kingdom of heaven</u>:…*- Matthew 16:18-19

It's only natural that Peter would be the one explaining how to receive the power, based on the proclamation of Jesus himself.

The point here is that you must interpret scripture with other scripture. If everything does not mesh together, then you are misinterpreting something. James explains to us that believing (faith) in and of itself is not enough. Even the devils believe. If you truly believe in something, you will act (do works) on that belief…

*Even so faith, if it hath not works, is dead, being alone. 18 Yea, a man may say, Thou hast faith, and I have works: shew me thy faith without thy works, and I will shew thee my faith by my works. 19 Thou believest that there is one God; thou doest well: the devils also believe, and tremble.* – James 2:17-19

If you truly believe on and receive Jesus Christ as your Lord and savior, you will do the works of repenting, being baptized, and receiving the Holy Ghost as taught by Peter. It is the action behind your belief that proves you truly believe.

Another example would be scriptures such as…

*For <u>by grace are ye saved through faith</u>; and that not of yourselves: it is the gift of God: 9 <u>Not of works</u>, lest any man should boast.* – Ephesians 2:8-9

Some people refuse to accept that repentance and baptism are essential to receiving the Holy Ghost because these are works or actions. If that were true, then Acts 2:38 would be wrong! We've already seen that faith or belief leads to works or obedience. Therefore we can see that this scripture is teaching us that the works themselves are not what save us. We are unworthy of this wonderful gift from God and there is nothing we can do to earn it. However, this doesn't negate the fact that in order to receive it you must act.

Consider a grandson who lived out of town that you wished you could get to know better. You call him up and ask him to visit you for a month during summer break. You share some of the fun things that you could do together and mention some of the gifts that you intend to lavish on him if he comes. You aren't trying to bribe him to come, you just want to share your love with him. In order to receive any of this, the grandson has to choose to go. It's important to understand that his action in going doesn't mean he is earning the blessings you promised him. This is what the Apostle Paul is telling us in Ephesians. God is willing to save us if we will just come to him, but the process of our coming certainly doesn't earn his blessings.

As you look at the entirety of the Bible, you will find that every verse talking about receiving power, or being saved, or having eternal life either supports Acts 2:38, or is additional information to help you understand the full extent of Acts 2:38. Having that in mind, let's see just what this verse is trying to tell us…

## Repent

Some people struggle with the idea of repentance. They feel that they are a good person and who has the right to say otherwise. What we must understand is that we don't set the standard. God's ideals are much higher than ours. He considers hatred equal to murder (1 John 3:15), lust to adultery (Matthew 5:28), and disobedience to witchcraft (1 Samuel 15:23). Isaiah tells us that even our good deeds are nothing to brag about...

*...we are all as an unclean thing, and <u>all our righteousnesses</u> are as filthy rags;...* - Isaiah 64:6

This is why the Bible tells us that...

*...all have sinned, and come short of the glory of God;* - Romans 3:23

Not only do we have to believe and receive Christ in order to apply Acts 2:38 to our lives, we can never be truly repentant unless we come to the understanding that we are sinners who are unacceptable before God.

Many people feel that repentance is simply feeling sorry for the wrong things that they have done in their lives. True repentance goes beyond just feeling sorry. True repentance drives a change of heart, mind, and/or attitude.

The Greek word that was translated to repent in Acts 2:38 means *"to think differently or afterwards, that is, reconsider (morally to feel compunction)"* [1].

One of Webster's definitions of repent, specifically in reference to theology, is *"to sorrow or be pained for sin, as a violation of God's holy law, a dishonor to his character and government, and the foulest ingratitude to a Being of infinite benevolence."* [2].

John the Baptist was called the fore runner of Christ. His main message was repentance. He told the people that he needs to see evidence of their repentance by a change of lifestyle…

*Bring forth therefore fruits meet for repentance*: - Matthew 3:8

In this verse, fruits is referring to evidence as noted in the Contemporary English Version of this same verse…

*Do something to show that you have really given up your sins.* – Matthew 3:8 (CEV)

So what are we supposed to do if we are truly repentant? First we need to understand that we are sinners, who have hurt God by our wrong doing, and be sorry about it…

*For godly sorrow worketh repentance to salvation…* - 2 Corinthians 7:10

Secondly, we need to admit our sins before God…

*If we <u>confess</u> our sins, he is faithful and just to forgive us our sins, and to cleanse us from all unrighteousness.* – 1 John 1:9

Finally, it's necessary to do your absolute best to stop sinning. This is a part of our never ending quest for perfection that was mentioned earlier…

*He that covereth his sins shall not prosper: but whoso confesseth <u>and forsaketh</u> them shall have mercy.* - Proverbs 28:13

True repentance is understanding that change is necessary in your life, doing your best to make those changes, and making amends to those you have wronged. It's God's grace that allows us to come to a place of repentance, but we must come…

*The Lord is not slack concerning his promise, as some men count slackness; but is longsuffering to us-ward, not willing that any should perish, but that all should come to repentance.* – 2 Peter 3:9

## Be Baptized

For those not raised in Christianity, baptism may seem rather strange. Why would you go through a ceremony in front of a group of people where you get all wet? What is the point? When we understand the true purpose of baptism, and what it does for us, it's easy to see why you want to be baptized. The Bible tells us that baptism accomplishes a number of things...

## Take on or apply Christ's burial to our lives

*Therefore we are buried with him [Jesus] by baptism into death...* - Romans 6:4 (also see Colossians 2:12)

As noted earlier, Jesus paid the price to cover our sins (John 3:16). What is often referred to as the good news, or the gospel, is that He died, was buried, and came to life again so that we could have a relationship with Him (I Corinthians 15:1-4, Romans 1:16). It's that relationship that allows the power of God to work in us.

Romans 6 and Colossians 2 show how Acts 2:38 is a symbolic partaking of Christ's death, burial, and resurrection. Jesus died physically; we die spiritually by dying out to sin through repentance. Jesus was buried physically; we are buried spiritually in baptism. Jesus rose from the dead; we receive new life when receiving the Holy Ghost, commonly referred to as being born again (See John chapter 3). By following Acts 2:38, we are essentially applying the gospel to our life.

## Baptism washes our sins away

*And now why tarriest thou? arise, and be baptized, and*

*wash away thy sins, calling on the name of the Lord.* – Acts 22:16

Acts 2:38 tells us to 'repent and be baptized…for the remission of sins.' By being baptized, after having truly repented, our sins are remitted or forgiven. They are washed away from our lives, making us clean before God.

### Gives us a clear conscience

*…But baptism is more than just washing your body. It means turning to God with a clear conscience, because Jesus Christ was raised from death.* - 1 Peter 3:21 (CEV)

Here we see again where the Bible ties a component of Acts 2:38 (baptism) to Christ's death, burial, and resurrection. The two go together hand in hand. By doing our part, we can freely approach God with a clear conscience, likely because we are obeying God's expectations and addressing the sin in our lives.

### Baptism saves us

*He that believeth and is baptized shall be saved; but he that believeth not shall be damned.* - Mark 16:16 (also see John 3:5, 1 Peter 3:20-21)

To this point we have not had a conversation on what it means to be saved. Biblical salvation is the concept of being rescued from the eternal punishment of sin. By addressing the sin in our lives, and turning ourselves to God, we can have a relationship with Him that will last for eternity. However, if we do not address the sin in our lives, then our sin stands between us and God, making us unfit to be in His presence. Salvation results in heaven while not being saved results in death, hell, and the grave.

Since Baptism is a component of salvation, it is also required...

*Can any man forbid water, that these should not be baptized, which have received the Holy Ghost as well as we? 48 And <u>he commanded them</u> to be baptized in the name of the Lord. Then prayed they him to tarry certain days.* - Act 10:47-48

Repentance and baptism go hand in hand. Once you die out to sin, the Bible tells us to bury it, but you can't bury what isn't dead. Repentance without baptism means our sins are still tied to our life in some manner. Baptism without repentance means nothing, because we are still living in our sin.

Now that we have explained what baptism is let's look at how to be baptized...

## Immersion

Some people baptize by sprinkling or pouring water over someone. While this may be more convenient, you cannot call this baptism as it does not meet the definition of the word. The word baptize comes from the original Greek word baptizo which means 'to make whelmed (that is, fully wet)'[1]. To whelm is 'to cover with water or other fluid; to cover by immersion in something that envelops on all sides;'[2]. Biblical baptism is without question, the complete immersion of someone in water. Since baptism is a symbolic burial, it would only make sense that the person is put completely under the surface, just like a physical burial.

## In Jesus Name

*Neither is there salvation in any other* [Jesus Christ of Nazareth]*: for there is none other name under heaven given among men, whereby we must be saved.* – Acts 4:12

Since baptism is applying the death of Christ to our lives, it only makes sense that we would be baptized in His name, as called out in Acts 2:38. Baptism in Jesus name is called out, implied, or administered in a number of verses: Luke 24:47, Acts 10:48, 8:16, 19:5, I Corinthians 1:13, Colossians 3:17

There is one verse in the Bible that may seem to

contradict this practice...

*Go ye therefore, and teach all nations, baptizing them in the name of the Father, and of the Son, and of the Holy Ghost:* - Matthew 28:19

So why would Jesus himself give us a different strategy for baptism than what we see in the rest of the Bible? He wouldn't. Therefore we should seek to understand what Christ was telling us in this verse.

First off, Jesus didn't give us any names, He gave us titles. You can't cash a check that is simply signed with a title, you need to have a name. Likewise in baptism, we must apply the name to our lives. We know the name of the Son is Jesus, referring to himself. What are the names of the Father and the Holy Ghost? In John 5:43 Jesus says 'I am come in my Father's name.' In John 14:26 Jesus says that the Holy Ghost shall be sent in his name. While this subject is a book in and of itself, what Jesus was telling us in this verse is that Father, Son, and Holy Spirit are not separate entities but one, and that the man Christ Jesus is our mediator to God, giving us His name to apply...

*For there is one God, and one mediator between God and men, the man Christ Jesus;* - 1 Timothy 2:5 (Also see Hebrews 8:6, 9:15, 12:24)

*Beware lest any man spoil you through philosophy and vain deceit, after the tradition of men, after the rudiments of the world, <u>and not after Christ</u>. 9 For <u>in him dwelleth all the fulness of the Godhead bodily</u>. 10 And ye are complete in him, which is the head of all principality and power:* - Colossians 2:8-10

So we can see that baptism is the immersion of a truly repentant person under water in the name of Jesus Christ. What do you do if you have already been baptized but you did not meet one of these three aspects? Get re-baptized…

*And he said unto them, Unto what then were ye baptized? And they said, Unto John's baptism. 4 Then said Paul, John verily baptized with the baptism of repentance, saying unto the people, that they should believe on him which should come after him, that is, on Christ Jesus. 5 When they heard this, they were baptized in the name of the Lord Jesus.* – Acts 19:3-5

## Receive the Holy Ghost

Acts 2:38 tells us that once we have repented and been baptized that we will receive the Holy Ghost. Is it automatic? Can we know without a doubt that we have received it? This one verse answers both questions…

*He* [Paul] *said unto them, Have ye received the Holy Ghost since ye believed?…* – Acts 19:2

Based on this one verse, it's quite obvious you don't receive the Holy Ghost automatically, whether it's believing, repenting, being baptized, or anything else because Paul would simply have asked them if they followed the steps. Secondly: This verse shows us that we can know that we have received it, or Paul wouldn't have asked the question. In Acts chapter 8, we actually find people seeking the Holy Ghost that have not yet received it...

*Now when the apostles which were at Jerusalem heard that Samaria had received the word of God, they sent unto them Peter and John: 15 Who, when they were come down, prayed for them, that they might receive the Holy Ghost: 16 (For as yet he was fallen upon none of them: only they were baptized in the name of the Lord Jesus.) 17 Then laid they their hands on them, and they received the Holy Ghost.* - Act 8:14 -17

So does this confirm that we can know without a doubt whether or not we have been filled with the Holy Ghost? If you read this entire story (Acts 8:5-25) you will see that a man named Simon witnessed what happened and offered money to be able to fill people with the Holy Ghost. Simon was believed to have great power of God because of his ability to work magic. Whether sleight of hand or through actual sorcery, this man amazed people with his abilities. It would require a lot more than something natural taking place to impress Simon;

obviously he was witnessing the supernatural.

So what did Simon see? Acts 8 doesn't tell us, but if we go back to the beginning in Acts 2, we see two and possibly three supernatural things take place…

*And when the day of Pentecost was fully come, they were all with one accord in one place. 2 And suddenly there came <u>a sound from heaven</u> as of a rushing mighty wind, and it filled all the house where they were sitting. 3 And there appeared unto them <u>cloven tongues like as of fire</u>, and it <u>sat upon each of them</u>. 4 And they were all filled with the Holy Ghost, and began to <u>speak with other tongues, as the Spirit gave them utterance</u>.* – Acts 2:1-4

**A sound from heaven** as of a rushing mighty wind appears to be a supernatural experience. However, it was not individualized and we never read of it happening again. This appears to be a one-time event.

**Cloven tongues like fire** setting on each of them is definitely individualized but this is also a one-time event that we never read of again.

**Speaking in tongues**, or speaking in a language that is unknown to the speaker, is supernatural, seen multiple times in the Bible, and continues today. Acts 10 confirms that speaking in tongues is the evidence…

RECEIVE POWER

*While Peter yet spake these words, the Holy Ghost fell on all them which heard the word....46 For they heard them speak with tongues, and magnify God.* - Act 10:44, 46

If you have never spoke in tongues before, seek a new level in your relationship with God today! Whether you have never known God or served Him all of your life, He wants to fill you with more of His power. Join the millions of others who have experienced the infilling of the Holy Ghost evidenced by speaking in an unknown language.

So how do you receive the Holy Ghost? It's simple...
1. Believe that Jesus Christ is God and that He died for your sins
2. Truly repent by confessing your sins and forsaking them
3. Be baptized by immersion in Jesus name
4. Ask God to fill you with the Holy Ghost
5. Worship and Praise God
6. Allow God to speak a different language through you (He will not force Himself on you)

Some receive the Holy Ghost immediately. For others it takes time. If you are actively seeking the Holy Ghost and not receiving it, don't give up. Live for God to the best of your ability and keep seeking. Ask yourself...
- Have I truly repented? Is there still sin in my life that I am not actively addressing?

- Is there someone that I should seek forgiveness from and/or make restitution with?
- Am I turning my life completely over to God?

Receiving the Holy Ghost is the greatest thing that can happen in your life! The power of God resides within you and helps you face whatever challenges life may throw at you. In addition to that, God has given us His Word (The Bible) which is filled with wisdom and understanding for living this life. Combine the power of the Holy Ghost with God's wisdom and you have an unbeatable combination!

*I can do all things through Christ which strengtheneth me.*
Philippians 4:13

# Power Over Insecurity

Sandy didn't have a chance from the start. By the time she was born, her father had already left her alcoholic mother, leaving them to fend for themselves. Sandy never met her father, but mom would often talk about him when drunk. He was a handsome and successful business man, which showed by the size of the child support payment that came faithfully each month. A lot of good the money did though. They eked out a living in poverty while mom drank the check away. Sandy couldn't be certain but she was pretty sure her mother hated her. She made it clear that the only reason dad left was because she had gotten pregnant, and therefore Sandy had destroyed her life. Her aunt confided to her once that mom was always a drunk and Sandy had nothing to do with dad's leaving, but it didn't help ease the dull ache of not being loved.

No matter what Sandy did, no matter how hard she tried, it was never good enough. Her mother treated her as if she were a useless burden. By the time she entered school she was so timid and socially maladjusted that all the other kids made fun of her. She was an outcast in society who learned to survive on her own.

Upon becoming a teenager Sandy's body began to fill out. For the first time in her life she started receiving positive attention. Some of it was not the attention she would prefer but at least they were interested in her. She began making friends, going to parties, hanging out, and having fun. Sure, the guys pushed her to do things she didn't want to, but it was a small price to pay for the attention she desperately desired. Some of the other girls called her names that hurt but what did that matter, they had been calling her names her whole life.

By the age of 21, Sandy had experienced everything in life that her friends said was fun. Over time though, the fun was getting less and less and the dull ache that she grew up with was growing stronger. After a string of broken relationships and failed efforts at holding a job, she knew she was drinking more than she should. She feared she was becoming just like her mother. Sandy felt worthless. Not only was her birth a mistake, she'd grown to truly believe that she herself was a mistake…

---

While Sandy's story is a fictional one, thousands of people have faced similar events in their lives, feeling inadequate and worthless. Insecurity can stem from numerous sources…

- Lack of Love
- Not fitting in with societies definition of success based on size, beauty, intelligence, financial status, social skills, etc
- Being degraded by others through teasing, bullying, ridiculing, etc
- High expectations from others
- Past failures
- And on and on…

While your story may seem minor compared to Sandy's, that doesn't make your struggle any easier. At its best, insecurity can hold you back from moving forward in your life. At its worse, it can lead to depression and even suicide.

No matter what circumstances lead to insecurity, the end result is a lack of self-confidence. It's important to understand that you can do amazing things through the power of the Holy Ghost!

*I can do all things through Christ which strengtheneth me.* – Philippians 4:13

Stand on the promise that you were made in God's image. No matter what others may say, no matter how you may feel, you were designed by God…

*So God created man in his own image, in the image of God created he him; male and female created he them.* – Genesis 1:27

*I will praise thee; for I am fearfully and wonderfully made* - Psalms 139:14

One of the major problems we face is measuring ourselves against society's standard. What the world thinks is important is nothing compared to what God designed you to be. The world values talent more than trust, beauty more than character, power more than integrity, and wealth more than wisdom. Teams will pay millions to someone who can catch a football. Fans will hang his poster on the wall and praise his ability. Kids dream of growing up to be like him. All this despite the fact that the player has no morals or character. Society wants to see him change for the better, but so long as he keeps catching the football, they really don't care.

Don't allow a messed up society to dictate whether or not you are worth anything! Don't put stock in the petty values of this world! Focus on what has eternal value…

*Lay not up for yourselves treasures upon earth, where moth and rust doth corrupt, and where thieves break through and steal: 20 But lay up for yourselves treasures in heaven, where neither moth nor rust doth corrupt, and where thieves do not break through nor steal: 21 For where your treasure is, there will your heart be also.* - Matthew 6:19-21

Some people allow their past wrongs to intimidate them from having a future. Sin leaves many feeling inadequate or afraid to try. People tend to judge us based on our past and we tend to think that God judges us the same way. The Bible tells us that God has cast our sins into 'the depths of the sea' (Micah 7:9) and that they are 'as far as the east is from the west' (Psalms 103:12). Paul committed atrocities against Christians and yet he became one of the greatest apostles in the New Testament. David committed adultery and then murdered the woman's husband and yet he is called a man after God's own heart (Acts 13:22). God does not judge us based on our start but rather our finish. If you have not done so already, repent of your past and move forward!

*My little children, these things write I unto you, that ye sin not. And if any man sin, we have an advocate with the Father, Jesus Christ the righteous:* – 1 John 2:1

Others are intimidated by their past mistakes and failures. They tried to accomplish something with their life and failed. Now they are afraid to try again. Failure should not define you, it should teach you. It is a powerful learning opportunity that should be used as a tool rather than something to hold us back. Thomas Edison is known for failing over 1000 times trying to create an economical incandescent light bulb. Because he did not give up, he brought light to the world.

Abraham Lincoln failed time and again, but because he did not give up, he was able to guide America through one of their darkest hours. In the Bible you will find many examples of failure. I believe God intentionally gave us these stories to teach us that everyone is human. We will all fail at points in our lives. Don't be afraid of failing, be afraid of not trying. Learn from your failures, press forward, and see how God can use you to change the world.

Others feel they can never measure up to the high expectations of others. While some people are taught that they will never amount to anything, others are pressured to be highly successful. Usually those that place these high expectations on someone have something specific in mind. It may be sports, taking over the family business, or pursuing a specific career. This can create high levels of insecurity within people, leaving them afraid to even try, or afraid to break away from those expectations to pursue their own desires. While some people are doing this with your best interests in mind, others are doing it for their own selfish motives. Either way, you need to understand that God designed you and His plan for your life may or may not have anything to do with what others think. Don't be afraid to pursue what you believe your purpose is, even if it's at the disappointment of others. Seek God's plan for your life and pursue it.

## RECEIVE POWER

*But seek ye first the kingdom of God, and his righteousness; and all these things shall be added unto you.* - Matthew 6:33

So how do you have power over insecurity?
- First: Receive the power of the Holy Ghost by following Acts 2:38
  (See 'How do I receive the power' chapter)
- Accept that you were fearfully and wonderfully made by God, in His image, with a purpose in mind. God does not make mistakes
- Don't allow society, friends, family, or even enemies to define you. Let God define you
- Pursue God's design for your life. This is where you will find true fulfilment and success

Jesus told a story commonly known as the parable of the talents. This parable can be found in Matthew 25:14-30. In the story, a master trusts three of his servants with three different amounts of money and then goes on a journey. He gave each servant an amount that they were capable of handling. When the master returned, two of the servants had invested his money wisely and were able to give him a return on his investment. The third servant admitted that he was afraid of failing his master and hid the money, which he then returned to him. The master praised the two servants who used what he gave them to generate a return but he rebuked the servant who did nothing out of fear.

can be a destructive and debilitating force. People who suffer with anxiety often struggle with things that most likely will never even happen. We can know in our heart and mind that there is nothing to fear and yet our body refuses to accept it. It can be damaging physically, mentally, socially and emotionally.

At the heart of anxiety is a fear of not being able to handle or cope with the situation. This is likely why many who suffer with anxiety also show signs of Obsessive Compulsive Disorder (OCD), as they attempt to exhibit control in their life. The problem is that with all of the external stimuli in this world, we have limited control over what happens to us. We can carefully look both ways before pulling out into traffic, but we have no guarantee that while we are watching for a safe opportunity to pull out that someone won't hit us from behind.

Science has shown that taking proper care of yourself can help those with mild anxiety. According to Psychology Today, "Habits such as exercising, sleeping well, and limiting the amount of caffeine and alcohol consumed can prove helpful."[6] Taking care of your body is a Biblical concept. Our body is the temple of the Holy Ghost and therefore we are called to care for it appropriately (1 Corinthians 3:16-17, 6:19-20). There are many benefits to living a healthy lifestyle and God knew this when giving us the Bible.

While caring for our body is an important physical and spiritual concept which we all should strive to apply to our lives, for those who struggle with anxiety God has a much more important message for you...

*Trust in the LORD with all thine heart; and lean not unto thine own understanding. 6 In all thy ways acknowledge him, and he shall direct thy paths. –* Proverbs 3:5-6

We have limited control over what may happen to us but God has full control! Whatever takes place in our lives, He either dictates or allows it. If we stop worrying about what is out of our control and give it completely to the Lord, He will take care of us!

*And he [Jesus] said unto his disciples, Therefore I say unto you, Take no thought for your life, what ye shall eat; neither for the body, what ye shall put on. 23 The life is more than meat, and the body is more than raiment. 24 Consider the ravens: for they neither sow nor reap; which neither have storehouse nor barn; and God feedeth them: how much more are ye better than the fowls? 25 And which of you with taking thought can add to his stature one cubit? 26 If ye then be not able to do that thing which is least, why take ye thought for the rest? 27 Consider the lilies how they grow: they toil not, they spin not; and yet I say unto you, that Solomon in all his glory was not arrayed like one of these. 28 If then God so clothe*

*the grass, which is to day in the field, and to morrow is cast into the oven; how much more will he clothe you, O ye of little faith? 29 And seek not ye what ye shall eat, or what ye shall drink, neither be ye of doubtful mind. 30 For all these things do the nations of the world seek after: and your Father knoweth that ye have need of these things. 31 <u>But rather seek ye the kingdom of God; and all these things shall be added unto you</u>.* – Luke 12:22-31

God takes care of nature and the animals. You are much more important to him than these. Seek God and he will take care of you!

*Aren't two sparrows sold for only a penny? But your Father knows when any one of them falls to the ground. 30 Even the hairs on your head are counted. 31 So don't be afraid! You are worth much more than many sparrows.* – Matthew 10:29-31 (CEV)

The key to overcoming anxiety is to trust the Lord with your life. Give him complete control. Yes: We are called to make wise decisions and not simply plunge into life foolishly. We should strive to control the things in our lives that we have control over, considering God's desires as we do so. But the rest we need to give to Him.

*Don't worry about anything, but pray about everything. With thankful hearts offer up your prayers and requests to God. 7 Then, because you belong to Christ Jesus, God will bless you with peace that no one can completely understand. And this peace will control the way you think and feel.* - Philippians 4:6-7 (CEV)

It is important that we completely trust God. We must believe (have faith) that he will be there for us. You cannot use your past or current circumstances to dictate whether or not God will be there for you. God sees the big picture while we only see a small piece. There is probably no better place where this is portrayed than in the book of Job. As Job faced horrible suffering in his life, he had so much faith in God that he made the statement, *"Though he slay me, yet will I trust in him"* (Job 13:15). Seek God and have faith that he will take care of you…

*Now faith is the substance of things hoped for, the evidence of things not seen…But without faith it is impossible to please him: for he that cometh to God must believe that he is, and that he is a rewarder of them that diligently seek him.* - Hebrews 11:1,6

When I'm lying in bed, feeling anxious about my chest pain, I have found that the only thing that helps is calling on the name of Jesus. Sometimes I will get up and go in the other room and other times I will just lay in bed and pray quietly, calling on His name. When I completely let go and trust in God, a peace washes over me and any fear that I have disappears. Even if it will be my last night on earth, I am comforted knowing that my life is in God's hands, and nobody cares for me more than He does.

# POWER OVER ANXIETY

I'm usually asleep within minutes…

So how do you have power over anxiety?
- First: Receive the power of the Holy Ghost by following Acts 2:38
  (See 'How do I receive the power' chapter)
- Take care of yourself through proper diet, exercise, etc
- Seek God. Grow your relationship with him
- Make wise, prayerful, Biblical choices in the things that you can control
- Prayerfully and completely trust in the Lord with all of your heart in the things that you cannot control
- If anxiety starts to build up in your life, focus your mind on Jesus rather than the issue. Verbally call out His name as you mentally give your worry to Him

When weather conditions prevent a pilot from being able to see, they are forced to rely on their gauges to be safe. The problem takes place when a pilot becomes disoriented and their gauges do not match what their body is telling them. They struggle with whether to trust their gauges or their instincts. Their training tells them to trust the gauges but their body is screaming that the gauges are wrong. Fear and anxiety build as the pilot faces a life or death choice; Do they trust their training or their heart? Those that trust their training are fine while those who trust their heart, or become immobilized by fear, often die...

*For God hath not given us the spirit of fear; but of power, and of love, and of a sound mind.* – 2 Timothy 1:7

The Bible is our gauge which teaches us to not worry about our circumstances. Find peace and comfort by trusting God, seeking Him, and giving Him your problems. Don't trust your instincts, trust God. You can do it through the power of the Holy Ghost. God will be there for you!

*Could a mother forget a child who nurses at her breast? Could she fail to love an infant who came from her own body? <u>Even if a mother could forget, I will never forget you</u>.* - Isaiah 49:15 (CEV)

*Casting all your care upon him; for he careth for you.* - 1 Peter 5:7

# Power Over Depression

Nathan was a typical kid who lived a relatively normal life. He had friends in the neighborhood that he enjoyed playing with each day. He attended the local school where he made good grades and got along well with his teachers. Life wasn't great, it wasn't bad, it was just life. Being a child, he didn't question life, he just lived it...

But when Nathan was eight years old his world was turned upside down. His grandparents, whom he'd never met before, showed up and took him away. Ripping him from the only life he knew, he found himself plunged into a world of darkness. His parents were suddenly gone and no longer a part of his life. He lived over three hours from home so he had no friends. His grandparents were complete strangers to him and he felt no love from them. He was filled with confusion and had nobody to turn to. His Grandma tried to be a good mother, but due to her age and health she could barely take care of herself. Grandpa had his own interests and hardly paid attention to him. Nathan would roam the streets alone. Over time he came to know a number of kids around his age, but none of them were a good influence. Nathan quickly became an angry, bitter, and depressed child. At the age of 12, he came close to joining a gang.

But at the age of thirteen, Nathan was introduced to Christianity and received the Holy Ghost. God took away the pain and filled him with exuberance and passion. He became actively involved in the church and has been ever since. But despite the change in his life, he still struggled with some depression and bitterness over his parent's abandonment. The power of the Holy Ghost had delivered him in an amazing way but the pain wasn't gone completely. At the age of seventeen, Nathan realized that it was up to him to let it go. He completely forgave his parents, giving all of his bitterness, frustrations, and depression to God. He refused to focus on the past, and chose to focus on only positive aspects of his parents. Nathan learned to love his parents all over again, he has a good relationship with them today, and has been completely free from depression ever since…

---

Depression can strike anyone. While often triggered by negative or stressful events in life, some people can face horrible situations and not become depressed while others can seemingly have everything going for them and yet struggle with depression.

While God may allow us to go through bouts of depression in order to mold us into a stronger person, we can rest in the fact that He does not want us to stay there. Jesus came to help us live life to the fullest…

*I am come that they might have life, and that they might have it more abundantly.* – John 10:10

In Luke chapter 6, Jesus was telling his disciples that those who were poor, hungry and sad were blessed. Those that were hated and mistreated for following God were blessed. He went on to say that we should rejoice when we are hurting because we know it's only temporary…

*Rejoice ye in that day, and leap for joy: for, behold, your reward is great in heaven…* – Luke 6:23

The power of positive thinking has probably been understood throughout time, and has even been taken to extremes in some circumstances. There is plenty of evidence indicating that people who portray a positive attitude tend to live healthier and happier lives, often despite their circumstances. This isn't so much a discovery by humankind as it is a gift from God. He designed our minds and bodies to react positively to a positive attitude. This also helps create a positive atmosphere around us, which in turn creates a better living environment. We see this truth evidenced throughout scripture…

## RECEIVE POWER

*My friends, be glad, even if you have a lot of trouble. 3 You know that you learn to endure by having your faith tested.* – James 1:2-3 (CEV)

We as Christians can have a positive outlook because we have a promise of hope…

*And we know that all things work together for good to them that love God…* - Romans 8:28

Being filled with the Holy Ghost, we can have joy in the fact that no matter what we go through, it will have a positive finish. People without God do not have that promise…

*If our hope in Christ is good only for this life, we are worse off than anyone else.* – 1 Corinthians 15:19 (CEV)

Jesus was our ultimate example of this. He chose to go through horrible suffering in order that we might have eternal life with Him. He endured pain and agony knowing that it would all be worth it in the end…

*Looking unto Jesus the author and finisher of our faith; who for the joy that was set before him endured the cross, despising the shame, and is set down at the right hand of the throne of God.* – Hebrews 12:2

One of the best ways to avoid depression in the first

place, or to escape it if you are in it, is by changing your overall attitude and what you choose to focus your mind on[7]...

*Don't be like the people of this world, but let God change the way you think...* - Romans 12:2

The world focuses on pleasing self, which at best can only bring temporary happiness. God teaches us that true peace, joy, and contentment comes by focusing on pleasing Him and by making a difference in the lives of others. Paul continues his prior conversation by providing us with examples on how we can do that...

*God has also given each of us different gifts to use. If we can prophesy, we should do it according to the amount of faith we have. 7 If we can serve others, we should serve. If we can teach, we should teach. 8 If we can encourage others, we should encourage them. If we can give, we should be generous. If we are leaders, we should do our best. If we are good to others, we should do it cheerfully...10 Love each other as brothers and sisters and honor others more than you do yourself...13Take care of God's needy people and welcome strangers into your home. 14 Ask God to bless everyone who mistreats you. Ask him to bless them and not to curse them. 15 When others are happy, be happy with them, and when they are sad, be sad. 16 Be friendly with everyone. Don't be proud and feel that you are smarter than others. Make friends with ordinary people. 17 Don't mistreat someone who has mistreated you. But try to earn the respect of others, 18 and do your best to live at peace with everyone.* - Romans 12:6-18 (CEV)

Turn your focus outward. Reach out to others. Challenge yourself to make a difference for God or in someone else's life. Reach out to someone less fortunate than you to not only bless them, but to also help realize how blessed you are.

I was listening to the radio the other day and they were talking about depression. The person the announcer was talking with made an interesting statement. He said when you are feeling depressed to read a Psalm aloud. David endured many hardships. Often in the Psalms you see him bring his complaints and struggles before God. In the end though, David always ends up praising and trusting in God. Next time you are feeling down, open up to the Psalms, read a chapter aloud, and meditate on the message.

It was many years ago that I read the poem 'Footprints' for the first time in my life (Also known as 'Footprints in the sand'. Authorship disputed and thus unknown[8]). Even as a child, I was inspired by its words. We can go through periods in life where we feel absolutely and utterly alone, without hope and without a future. It's at those points that we can choose to despair or choose to trust God. If we pursue God, He will be with us, even if we don't feel like He is…

*…I am with you alway, even unto the end of the world…*
- Matthew 28:20

So how do you have power over depression?
- First: Receive the power of the Holy Ghost by following Acts 2:38
  (See 'How do I receive the power' chapter)
- Be comforted, knowing that your pain is only temporary
- Have a positive outlook on life. God is working it for good.
- Have an attitude of thankfulness
- Remind yourself that God is always there for you, even when it doesn't feel like it
- Turn your focus outward
- Praise God despite your circumstances…

There is a true story in the Bible about two apostles named Paul and Silas which can be found in Acts 16:16-36. In the process of spreading the gospel, Paul cast a demon out of a woman, freeing her from the spiritual oppression she was under. The demon had given this woman the power of divination, which was most likely the ability to foretell future events or bring out hidden secrets. At this time in history, women tended to be treated more like property than people. Some men were selfishly using her demon possession for their own financial gain, and when they found out that their source of income had been cut off, they falsely accused Paul and Silas in order to have them punished. Paul and Silas were beaten, thrown into prison, and locked in stocks.

Here they were, most likely in a filthy, stinky, rat infested, pitch black prison in the middle of the night. They were locked up in an uncomfortable position and were certainly bloody and in great pain. If anyone had a right to be depressed it was these two men. But rather than focus on their circumstances, Paul and Silas prayed and started singing praises to God loud enough for the other prisoners to hear.

God heard their praises and worked a miracle that night. An earthquake hit the prison, opening every door and releasing every bond. Not only did God work in Paul and Silas' life that night, but He showed his power to everyone in that prison. The keeper of the prison dedicated his life to the Lord, and it appears that his entire family did also.

God can use both positive and negative circumstances in your life to accomplish amazing things. When life is getting you down, and you feel yourself being drawn into that deep hole of depression, get your focus off of your own situation and on the greatness of God. Refuse to think about the negative but rather on the positive. Praise God in your circumstance and watch what He can do through it...

*Finally, brethren, whatsoever things are true, whatsoever things are honest, whatsoever things are just, whatsoever things are pure, whatsoever things are lovely, whatsoever things are of good report; if there be any virtue, and if there be any praise, think on these things.* – Philippians 4:8

# Power Over Addiction

Cindy was 9 years old when she joined a gang. With two local gangs in the neighborhood, venturing outside was a risk even for children. The only way to walk the streets in somewhat safety was to join one of the gangs for protection. While gang members treat each other as family, they generally encourage behavior that most families would be against. Cindy experienced things as an adolescent that parents pray their children never face. As both a coping mechanism and an expectation of the gang, she quickly turned to substance abuse. By the tender age of 11, Cindy was addicted to cigarettes, drugs, and alcohol.

Fast forward to the age of 35. The gang life was behind her but the pain from a life of neglect, abuse, and addiction were as strong as ever. Drugs and alcohol were her only means of escape. "Years of searching for a way out left her broken and bewildered". While painting an apartment one day, she carefully planned her suicide. It was important that she take her four children with her. She loved them too much to have them "suffer through the horrible pattern of life that she had lived before them". She must protect them in the only way she knew how...[18]

---

Addictions of any type can destroy families and destroy lives. They seem impossible to break, hence the term addiction. The body craves to be fed with whatever the person is addicted to. Some people refuse to admit they have a problem, or are unwilling to change, but for those who truly want to break free of addiction there is hope.

Having the power of the Holy Ghost in your life is key to being delivered from substances that control you. Some people are miraculously delivered when they receive the Holy Ghost while others are not. Why God chooses to free some immediately while others have to work at it is hard to know and likely varies with each situation. You can rest assured though that through the power of the Holy Ghost, you can break your bondage of addiction. It may not be easy, but if you are serious about it, God will help you.

The first step is admitting you have a problem, both to yourself and others. There is something about humbling one's self through verbal confession that allows the deliverance process to start. It's similar to exposing a festering wound so you can start treating it...

RECEIVE POWER

*He that covereth his sins shall not prosper: but whoso <u>confesseth and forsaketh</u> them shall have mercy.* - Proverbs 28:13

This can be extremely difficult, especially if it is a hidden addiction that nobody is aware of. Confession requires someone to confess to. First we need to confess to God but we also need to share our struggles with others. Depending on the situation, you should use wisdom and get guidance on who to confess to and how far reaching your confession should go. In most circumstances, you should confess to those that have been affected by your addiction, and to those that can help you at a minimum.

For those that have been affected by your addiction, it is important that you seek their forgiveness. You need to be truly repentant for the pain and trouble that you have caused as a result of your selfish indulgences. Depending on how strained the relationship is, this may not come immediately, or may have to be done in steps. But in most situations, it is important that this is eventually addressed.

*if you are about to place your gift on the altar and remember that someone is angry with you, 24 leave your gift there in front of the altar. Make peace with that person, then come back and offer your gift to God.* - Matthew 5:23-24 (CEV)

Secondly, it is critical to get help. Because of the shame that often accompanies addiction, many people try again and again to conquer it on their own, which almost never works. We need people in our lives to support, encourage, and help us through the recovery process. We also need someone that we can hold ourselves accountable to, who will commit to faithfully working with us as often as necessary.

When you receive the Holy Ghost, you automatically become a part of the body of Christ (1 Corinthians 12:27). This 'body' is referring to one another, or all those that are saved. We can look at it in the macro view, and understand that everyone who has received the Holy Ghost is part of a huge group, or body, but we also tend to look at it in the micro view, as each church or fellowship is a body within the body. The reason I bring this up is because we are called to be here for one another…

*And whether one member suffer, all the members suffer with it; or one member be honoured, all the members rejoice with it.* - 1Corinthians 12:26

1 Corinthians 12 talks about how we are all in one body, but we each have different gifts and talents to support the body. There are people in your church that can help you overcome your addiction. Work through your pastor and find them. If you attend a

smaller church, it may be necessary to solicit help from another church. They can also help you decide whether professional help is necessary.

Now that you have a team of support you need to be intentional about how to overcome your addiction. You cannot just want to change, you have to commit to change by taking action. Work with your team and come up with various strategies. This plan starts with a mental commitment…

*I made a covenant with mine eyes; why then should I think upon a maid?* – Job 31:1

Whatever your addiction is, you need to commit yourself to not focusing on it. This can be very difficult as most addictions attack our mind. One of the best ways to get your mind off of your addiction is to get it focused on something else…

*Set your affection on things above, not on things on the earth.* - Colossians 3:2

One of the most important things to focus on is God: Read the Bible, meditate on God's word, pray, fast, listen to sermons, get on fire for God, etc…

*If my people, which are called by my name, shall <u>humble themselves</u>, and <u>pray</u>, and <u>seek my face</u>, and <u>turn from their wicked ways</u>; then will I hear from heaven, and will* *forgive their sin, and will heal their land.* – 2 Chronicles 7:14

*This I say then, Walk in the Spirit, and ye shall not fulfil the lust of the flesh.* – Galatians 5:16

In order to keep your mind off of your addiction, create a plan to avoid temptation in the first place. Some examples would be…

If you cannot control what you view on the internet then get a good filter. If the filter isn't enough then create a plan where you can only be on the internet in public places, where people can see what you are viewing. If that isn't enough then get rid of your internet access completely. Yes: It is possible to survive without internet.

You need to clear your home of temptation. A recovering alcoholic cannot have beer for cooking, or wine to settle ones stomach. Make your home a safe place…

*Neither shalt thou bring an abomination into thine house, lest thou be a cursed thing like it: but thou shalt utterly detest it, and thou shalt utterly abhor it; for it is a cursed thing.* - Deuteronomy 7:26

If you are addicted to something that your friends do or that is prevalent in places that you go, then it's necessary to make new friends and to stop going to those places. Alcoholics can't break their addiction if they hang out at the bar. Even restaurants that serve alcohol may be too much of a temptation. Commit yourself to avoiding the temptation to start with! Being in proximity to what you are addicted to is dangerous. Don't fool yourself with the lie that you can handle it. Stay away.

You need to be especially cautious when you are emotional. Anger, stress, frustration, depression, etc, all tend to push you towards your addiction. Your mind will justify that you deserve a release due to your circumstances, or you simply won't care because of your emotional state. This will happen. Have a plan ahead of time for how to address it.

Up to this point we have been discussing strategies to minimize temptation but what happens when you are struggling? Temptation will come. The goal is to flee the temptation…

*<u>Flee</u> also youthful <u>lusts</u>: but follow righteousness, faith, charity, peace, with them that call on the Lord out of a pure heart.* -2 Timothy 2:22

Remember, addiction is generally a mind struggle. When struggling with temptation, you need strategies to help you re-focus your mind. One good option is to memorize key verses that you find helpful in relation to your addiction. These may be directly related or not. When you find yourself struggling, start quoting verses in your mind, or even out loud if necessary. For example…

General: *Submit yourselves therefore to God. Resist the devil, and he will flee from you.* – James 4:7

Drugs: *If any man defile the temple of God, him shall God destroy; for the temple of God is holy, which temple ye are.* – 1 Corinthians 3:17

Alcohol: *Wine is a mocker, strong drink is raging: and whosoever is deceived thereby is not wise.* – Proverbs 20:1

Pornography: *I will set nothing wicked before my eyes; I hate the work of those who fall away; It shall not cling to me.* – Psalms 101:3 (NKJV)

Sex: *Flee fornication. Every sin that a man doeth is without the body; but he that committeth fornication sinneth against his own body. 19 What? know ye not that your body is the temple of the Holy Ghost which is in you, which ye have of God, and ye are not your own?* – 1 Corinthians 6:18-19

Think about those you hurt when caught up in your addiction. If you truly care about them, you will not want to hurt them more than you already have. Don't let your mind trick you into thinking that this one time won't matter.

## RECEIVE POWER

Do something: Get your mind off of the temptation by focusing on a task, preferably with people that you would never give into your addiction in front of. There is an old saying that 'idle hands are the devil's workshop.' The Living Bible translation even uses this verbiage in Proverbs 16:27[12]. If your hands are busy accomplishing something, your mind is focused on the task at hand, greatly reducing temptation. Don't just expect ideas to jump out at you when you are struggling with temptation, have a plan ahead of time and then follow your plan. Obviously you don't want to get involved with something that turns into other problems in the future. Be wise in your choices.

Have a list of people that you can contact when struggling with your desires. Once again, if you try to cope yourself, you will most likely give in. Call on them! Don't be ashamed. Don't feel like you are being a burden. Get the help and encouragement you need when you need it most.

Finally: If you blow it and give into the temptation, don't let it destroy you. Get back up and keep going. Confess your failure to those who are supporting you. DO NOT hide it from them. You need them even more in these times and if you fail to disclose your failure to them you are likely to fall back into your addiction again.

POWER OVER ADDICTION

So how do you have power over addiction?
- First: Receive the power of the Holy Ghost by following Acts 2:38
  (See 'How do I receive the power' chapter)
- Confess your addiction to those you have hurt and those that can help
- Seek forgiveness from those you have hurt as a result of your addiction
- Get help
- Be intentional. Have a plan
- Pursue your relationship with God
- Remove sources of temptation from your life
- Do something. Keep your mind active on other things
- Flee temptation when it does come
- Don't give up

One thing that we didn't cover up to this point is the importance of finding any underlying sources for your addiction. Addictions are often coping mechanisms for deeper problems. You may drink to flee the stress in your life. You may do drugs to deaden the pain of your past. You may shop for a sense of accomplishment or self-worth. You may turn to pornography as an escape from challenging relationships. The list is endless. If you don't identify and address the source of your addiction, you will likely not break it. Your support team can help you with both.

God intervened on that fateful day Cindy was finalizing her suicide plans. The woman who would be moving into the apartment she was painting stopped by to see how it was progressing. This young woman was filled with the power of the Holy Ghost and Cindy was drawn to God's presence in the room. By the end of the visit the two had agreed to do a Bible study together. Within a short time Cindy was baptized and received the Holy Ghost for herself. Her life was so radically transformed by the love and power of God in her life that four months went by before it dawned on her that she had been miraculously healed of her addictions. In her words, "Jesus was the peace that I had been so desperate to find"[18]

Allow the power of the Holy Ghost to transform your life today!

Read Cindy's book titled "Get with the program | God's Program | A Christian perspective of Alcoholism and Drug Addiction" by Cynthia T. Adams, Insignia Publications

# Power Over Suffering

Cherry was excited about the new addition that they were adding on to their home. The extra space was just what they needed for their growing family. Her husband was up on the roof laying shingles one day when he called for her help. Not one to waste any time, his hammer blows continued as she made her way over to the ladder. Just as she stuck her head through a hole in the roof something slammed her in the eye. Her husband looked up and screamed "You've got a nail in your eye!" They both made it down the ladder to the ground floor where her husband innocently pulled the nail out.

Fluid was oozing from the wound in her eye. Her husband was very upset and wanted to rush her to the hospital. "Let me go into the bedroom first and pray", she said. As she sought the Lord, the power of the Holy Ghost moved into the room with her in a mighty way. Cherry felt impressed that if she could still see out of her eye when she opened it, that she should trust God for her healing. Although a good amount of fluid had drained out, she could still see. Her heart was filled with faith and thanksgiving as she worshipped God, speaking in tongues as the power of the Holy Ghost flowed through her. She knew that God was going to take care of her.

Much to her husband's disgust, they did not go to the hospital. Within four days, Cherry's eye was back to normal, with no infection or deterioration in her sight. God had completely healed her.

---

One of the age old questions in theology is 'why do bad things happen to good people.' While a Godly, healthy and cautious lifestyle can help avoid many trials, nobody is immune from the hardships that life has to offer. Humanity struggles with why a good God would allow people to suffer and many who have gone through severe pain, sickness, trials, and hardship have become angry and bitter with God.

Obviously God's intention for allowing pain and suffering in your life is not to make you bitter against him. God loves you so much that he became human to die a cruel and agonizing death, just so he could spend eternity with you (John 3:16). The last thing he wants is to have you turn against him. So we ask ourselves: If Jesus came so we could live an abundant life (John 10:10), why would we ever have to suffer? If the Holy Ghost is designed to give us power (Acts 1:8), why can we feel so powerless when we suffer? While we will never have the full answer to these questions here on earth, the Bible does give us some insights that can help us overcome our suffering as we go through it.

One reason for suffering is to help us grow stronger, giving glory to God in the process. The apostle Paul struggled with some type of ailment that he calls a 'thorn in the flesh.' We don't know what it was, but it was bad enough that Paul described it as a blow (buffet) from Satan himself. God refused to take it away from Paul, knowing that it would make him a better man…

*And <u>lest I should be exalted above measure</u> through the abundance of the revelations, there was given to me a thorn in the flesh, the messenger of Satan to buffet me, lest I should be exalted above measure. 8 For this thing I besought the Lord thrice, that it might depart from me. 9 And he said unto me, My grace is sufficient for thee: for <u>my strength is made perfect in weakness</u>. Most gladly therefore will I rather glory in my infirmities, that the power of Christ may rest upon me. 10 Therefore I take pleasure in infirmities, in reproaches, in necessities, in persecutions, in distresses for Christ's sake: for when I am weak, then am I strong.* – 2 Corinthians 12:7-10

Note that when Paul realized that his suffering was giving God glory, he became willing to continue in his pain. He also learned that his weakness helped make him a stronger person and therefore he appreciated the opportunity to suffer.

Another reason people suffer is because they are being persecuted for being followers of Christ. Horrible atrocities have been committed against Christians over the years. Here is an example of where the apostles were beaten just because they were talking in public to people about Jesus...

*...and when they had called the apostles, and beaten them, they commanded that they should not speak in the name of Jesus, and let them go. 41 And they departed from the presence of the council, rejoicing that they were counted worthy to suffer shame for his name. 42 And daily in the temple, and in every house, they ceased not to teach and preach Jesus Christ.* - Acts 5:40-42

The better understanding we have of the suffering that Christ took on for us, the easier it is to appreciate the opportunity to suffer in return for Him. The apostles were 'rejoicing that they were counted worthy to suffer for his name.' There are multiple examples in the Bible and scriptures about persecution to help inspire us to endure the suffering placed upon us with a positive attitude...

*Yet if any man suffer as a Christian, let him not be ashamed; but let him glorify God on this behalf.* – 1 Peter 4:16

*But and if ye suffer for righteousness' sake, happy are ye: and be not afraid of their terror, neither be troubled;...17*

*For it is better, if the will of God be so, that ye suffer for well doing, than for evil doing.* - 1Peter 3:14, 17

Persecution of any type brings pain and most of us are afraid of pain. That fear can cause us to make poor choices, giving in to peer pressure. Jesus reminds us to focus on the big picture…

*And fear not them which kill the body, but are not able to kill the soul: but rather fear him which is able to destroy both soul and body in hell.* - Matthew 10:28

Are you fully committed to serving God? To the point that you are willing to endure suffering, pain, and possibly even death for Him? If you aren't, chances are you will not serve him through any serious hardships. Allow the power of the Holy Ghost to give you the strength and commitment towards God that can carry you through anything!

Some people suffer simply because of time and chance. There is not a divine plan or reason behind it. It simply happens…

*I returned, and saw under the sun, that the race is not to the swift, nor the battle to the strong, neither yet bread to the wise, nor yet riches to men of understanding, nor yet favour to men of skill; but time and chance happeneth to them all.* – Ecclesiastes 9:11

RECEIVE POWER

There is a story of a blind man in the Bible whom Jesus healed. The disciples assumed that his blindness was a result of sin but Jesus said it was so people could see God's power at work...

*And as Jesus passed by, he saw a man which was blind from his birth. 2 And his disciples asked him, saying, Master, who did sin, this man, or his parents, that he was born blind? 3 Jesus answered, Neither hath this man sinned, nor his parents: but that the works of God should be made manifest in him.* - John 9:1-3

Did God cause this man to be born blind, just so he could show off his power years down the road as this verse implies? It's possible but not likely. In the CEV version Jesus states *"because of his blindness, you will see God work a miracle for him."*

Some people seem to fall into good things in life while others receive bad. It's not because God likes some more than others, it's just life. Life isn't fair. Some are born into wealth, health, and success while others are born into trials and hardships. The hand that life deals you is not nearly important as your attitude towards it. There are many extremely successful people in this world that are miserable and without hope while there are many people suffering each day that have peace, joy, and contentment in their lives.

I'm reminded of a dear friend in our church named Sandra (Sam) Bertram. At a young age, she was diagnosed with polio. Her body slowly deteriorated to where she could do less and less each year. For the last 10-15 years of her life, she spent most of her time in bed. During this time, my wife was blessed to be able to help care for Sam, so we got to know her better than most. Obviously Sam was human, with her good days and bad, but throughout her suffering she kept a positive attitude and we never saw her question God. In those latter years, Sam did not attend church often because of the pain involved with coming, but some days when she felt up to it she would be there. I remember more than once when the power of God would move through our services. People would be worshipping God though dancing, jumping, running, or whatever else they felt to do. Sam would drive her electric wheel chair to the front of the sanctuary and then spin in circles, worshipping God in her most exuberant way possible. Her pain and suffering could not drown out her joy in the Holy Ghost.

Finally, there is also the chance that some people may endure suffering simply because God chose to make them that way. This may seem cruel to some, but who are we to question God in his infinite wisdom?

*But, my friend, I ask, "Who do you think you are to question God? Does the clay have the right to ask the potter why he shaped it the way he did? 21 Doesn't a potter have the right to make a fancy bowl and a plain bowl out of the same lump of clay?"* – Romans 9:20-21 (CEV)

No matter why we suffer, it is important to stand upon God's promise that good will come from it...

*And we know that all things work together for good to them that love God, to them who are the called according to his purpose.* – Romans 8:28

We can trust that God will use our suffering for good, no matter what the reason behind it may be. Stand upon His promise! There is only one pre-requisite: Love God!

In all cases, our attitude towards suffering is of utmost importance. Allow it to turn your heart closer to God. Trust him to see you through your suffering and work positive change throughout. Imagine if we could see the big picture. We have no idea why God allows specific hardships in our lives. When we face him one day will we be ashamed of our reaction towards our suffering or will he say 'well done thou good and faithful servant'? Will we allow our suffering to make us better or bitter? It's our choice!

Time can seem to stand still when we suffer. Pain demands our attention and the more we focus on it, the slower time tends to move. Sometimes it feels like the pain will never go away. There is an old Persian adage[13] that says 'This too shall pass.' Time can be a healer, circumstances do change, and sometimes God miraculously delivers us from our affliction. However, others will suffer the rest of their lives. We need to understand that while it may seem like an eternity for us as mortals, from God's perspective it is a mere wisp in time. Our life is like the steam that rises from a tea kettle; it's here for a few seconds and then it's gone…

*Whereas ye know not what shall be on the morrow. For what is your life? It is even a vapour, that appeareth for a little time, and then vanisheth away.* – James 4:14

We live our life on God's schedule and he see's time completely different than we do…

*But, beloved, be not ignorant of this one thing, that one day is with the Lord as a thousand years, and a thousand years as one day.* – 2 Peter 3:8

So as you face suffering in this life comfort yourself with God's promise that it will pass. Without God you have hope in this life only but with God your hope is eternal. Even if you live your entire life without being delivered from your trial, you will then spend eternity free from suffering…

*And God shall wipe away all tears from their eyes; and there shall be no more death, neither sorrow, nor crying, neither shall there be any more pain: for the former things are passed away.* - Revelation 21:4

So how do you have power over suffering?
- First: Receive the power of the Holy Ghost by following Acts 2:38
(See 'How do I receive the power' chapter)
- Understand that you can grow through suffering
- Allow your suffering to turn you towards God rather than away
- Allow God to receive glory by the way you respond to your suffering and through your deliverance from it
- Understand that in light of eternity, our suffering is a wisp in time
- Maintain a positive attitude throughout

Last summer we took a family vacation. We stayed at an Airbnb which happened to be a duplex. During our time there we became friends with the family downstairs. One of them was Amber, a young lady in her twenties, who had been born blind. We got to know them better each day and by the end of the week I felt that it would be appropriate to ask Amber if we could pray for her to receive her sight. Her answer both surprised and inspired me. She said that many people had prayed for her over the years, and since God had not yet healed her, she believed her blindness was meant to be a part of who she was. She was not bitter about her disability, rather she was comfortable with it, believing there was a purpose behind it.

In our opening story, a young woman could have easily lost sight in only one of her eyes and yet God completely healed her within a few short days. Our closing story is about someone who has never been able to see and likely never will. Why would God choose to completely heal one person and yet allow the other to live their entire life in darkness? We will never know while here on this earth. What we do know is that God can be glorified by delivering us from suffering and by our response to it.

The Bible tells us that the fear of the Lord is the beginning of wisdom and knowledge (Psalms 111:10, Proverbs 9:10, 1:7). Isaiah shares how this wisdom and knowledge are the foundations that Jerusalem can stand upon during their trials. Their deliverance depends upon their Godly wisdom and knowledge, therefore they treasure their fear of the Lord…

*And wisdom and knowledge shall be the stability of thy times, and strength of salvation: the fear of the LORD is his treasure.* - Isaiah 33:6

The fear in these verses is referring to reverence, which is 'fear mingled with respect and esteem'[2]. If just for a moment we could see how great God is in comparison to our mortal lives, we would humbly fall before him in worship rather than question his motives. We would understand that God sees things on a level that we cannot comprehend...

*For my thoughts are not your thoughts, neither are your ways my ways, saith the LORD. 9 For as the heavens are higher than the earth, so are my ways higher than your ways, and my thoughts than your thoughts.* – Isaiah 55:8-9

Each of us have a choice when facing hardships. We can blame God, allowing it to destroy our relationship with him. Or we can fear God, grow in wisdom and character, and see God glorified all at the same time. Which will you choose?

*My friends, be glad, even if you have a lot of trouble. 3 You know that you learn to endure by having your faith tested. 4 But you must learn to endure everything, so that you will be completely mature and not lacking in anything. 5 If any of you need wisdom, you should ask God, and it will be given to you. God is generous and won't correct you for asking. 6 But when you ask for something, you must have faith and not doubt. Anyone who doubts is like an ocean wave tossed around in a storm....12 God will bless you, if you don't give up when your faith is being tested. He will reward you with a glorious life, just as he rewards everyone who loves him.* – James 1:2-6,12 (CEV)

# Power Over Anger

Years ago, MADtv put out a sketch starring Bob Newhart that became quite popular on YouTube. Commonly referred to as 'Stop It', this skit portrays Newhart as a counselor or therapist of some sort who is trying to help a young woman struggling with an irrational fear. Bob refused to dig into her past, or reasons why she may struggle with this fear, he simply told her to stop it.

While this skit was meant to be a comedy, which was a definite success, I believe one reason it became so popular is because they hit on a truth that affects almost everyone. Obviously some people have pasts that warrant counseling and help, but when it comes down to it, our reactions to life are a choice. We can choose to make positive choices, which tend to benefit ourselves and others, or we can make destructive choices.

People who struggle with anger hurt both themselves and others. Relationships are strained and some are either driven away, or choose to stay away. Those who stay in the relationship tend to find themselves walking on eggshells around the person, being cautious not to do or say anything that would ignite another outburst. Yes, your past may make it seemingly impossible, but through the power of the Holy Ghost it's time to stop allowing anger to control you.

*Cease from anger, and forsake wrath: fret not thyself in any wise to do evil.* - Psalms 37:8

King Solomon was the wisest man who ever lived (1 Kings 3:11-12). Solomon wrote the book of Proverbs, which is specifically designed to share wisdom and instruction to its readers (1:1-7). Here are some statements made in the book of Proverbs about anger (CEV)...

- *Fools think they know what is best, but a sensible person listens to advice. 16 Losing your temper is foolish; ignoring an insult is smart.* - 12:15-16
- *It's smart to be patient, but it's stupid to lose your temper.* - 14:29
- *People with bad tempers are always in trouble, and they need help over and over again. 20 Pay attention to advice and accept correction, so you can live sensibly.* - 19:19-20
- *If you churn milk you get butter; if you pound on your nose, you get blood-- and if you stay angry, you get in trouble.* - 30:33

I have struggled with anger myself. I remember once working on my car at my parents. I was getting very frustrated because it wasn't going well. I so much wanted to lose my temper and I was struggling to maintain my cool. In order to at least let off a little frustration, I threw my ratchet on the ground. As I did it, I was even feeling a little proud of myself for holding back as well as I was. However, in the process of throwing my ratchet on the ground, the extension that was attached came flying off and went straight through my parents' living room window.

Note the obvious from the Proverbs listed previously that losing your temper is foolish and creates more problems. There are few times that I have lost my temper and not regretted either what I did or said. Outbursts of anger do not improve problems, they create more.

But also note that in two of these four quotes that Solomon implies angry people do not listen to or heed advice from others. Anger is often a result of selfishness or pride and both of these character traits tend to ignore solid advice and justify negative behaviors. If you are serious about conquering your anger, then you need to be open to advice and criticism, and then follow it. You should also be proactive and seek out advice. Chances are people gave up trying to help you years ago and unless you solicit help they won't offer it. Humble yourself, admit your problem, listen, and make changes based on the advice given.

## RECEIVE POWER

We all get angry at times. Anger in and of itself is not necessarily wrong. What is important is how we react to our emotions. Ephesians 4:26 gives us a couple of good insights about anger…

*Be ye angry, and sin not: let not the sun go down upon your wrath:*

For those that struggle with anger, it may seem impossible to simply stop it. I remember being so angry once that I was ready to go into a rage. My heart had probably never beat faster, my adrenaline was peaked, and it took everything I could do to keep from lashing out. If someone had told me to stop it right at that point I probably would have hit them. I left the house before I did anything that would seriously damage my family. It took over ten minutes before my heartbeat started to slow down and probably half an hour before it was back to normal. After half an hour I was finally able to go back into the house. I was still keyed up, but I was back in control.

When we get angry we have a choice to make. Are we going to allow anger to control us or are we going to control our anger? One of the best ways to avoid it is to get away from the source before it's too late. There is a reason people say count to ten, or take three deep breaths. You need to step back from the situation and re-group. Leave if at all possible.

That doesn't mean you are running from your responsibilities, you may still need to face the issue, but you need to be able to face it in a calm manner...

*Run from temptations that capture young people. Always do the right thing. Be faithful, loving, and easy to get along with...* - 2 Timothy 2:22 (CEV)

Recognize the warning signs of anger and run from them. Take a break. Walk away. Schedule a later time to come back to the issue. Do whatever it takes to avoid an outburst. Be angry but don't sin.

The second part of Ephesians 4:26 says to not let the sun go down on your wrath. Controlling your anger does not mean hold it in and let it stew inside of you. You need to get beyond the anger as soon as possible. In the New Testament era, sundown was the beginning of a new day. God gave us a goal to set for ourselves. Don't allow your anger to be carried over into the next day. Do whatever it takes to address the issue in a way that your anger can be put behind you before you go to bed that night.

Another key step in having power over anger is to humble yourself and seek forgiveness from those that have experienced your outburst. There is something about true confession and repentance that makes you less likely to do it again...

*Therefore if thou bring thy gift to the altar, and there*

*rememberest that thy brother hath ought against thee; 24 Leave there thy gift before the altar, and go thy way; first be reconciled to thy brother, and then come and offer thy gift.* - Matthew 5:23-24

While these verses can stand on their own, stating that you should make amends with someone that you have hurt before you come before God, if you read the entire paragraph (verses 21-26) you will see that Jesus is specifically referring to people that have offended others in an unjust outburst of anger. When you have offended people by your anger, you need to do your best to make peace with them before approaching God. I promise you that the more you do this, the less often you will lose your temper.

Finally: Abide in God's love for you, practice loving others, and focus on God's will in your life. When you are caught up in God's love, and walking in his will, then if he allows something frustrating to come into your life, what call do you have to get angry over it? Secondly, if you truly love others, the last thing we want to do is hurt them with our selfish outbursts...

*Let all bitterness, and wrath, and anger, and clamour, and evil speaking, be put away from you, with all malice: 32 And be ye kind one to another, tenderhearted, forgiving one another, even as God for Christ's sake hath forgiven you.* - Ephesians 4:31-32

So how do you have power over anger?
- First: Receive the power of the Holy Ghost by following Acts 2:38
(See 'How do I receive the power' chapter)
- Understand that being angry is not a sin. Losing your temper is
- Losing your temper is foolish and only makes situations worse
- Seek criticism and advice. Listen to and apply it
- Get away from the situation, if at all possible, until you can control yourself
- Abide in God's love and will for your life. Love others
- Stop It. Don't allow anger to control you
- Humble yourself and make amends when you do blow it

As mentioned before, anger is often the result of selfishness. We get angry because we aren't getting what we want when we want it. If this is why we are getting angry, we need to stop it. If our anger is truly justified, we need to carefully choose how to react.

I've heard that anger does something to your brain, and the more you get angry, the harder it is not to get angry. I believe this because I have experienced it for myself. I catch myself patiently struggling with something that in the past would have caused me to throw a fit. It's as if God rewards us for seriously trying by re-wiring our brains. Learn to control your anger so when you are placed in a situation that you cannot walk away from, you will be able to get through it without regrets.

*Wherefore, my beloved brethren, let every man be swift to hear, slow to speak, slow to wrath: 20 For the wrath of man worketh not the righteousness of God.* - James 1:19

# Power In Relationships

Who doesn't struggle in a relationship somewhere?  If you don't live alone, there are periodic challenges in your home; from parents, to siblings, to roommates, to spouses, to children.  Even the pets can get on your nerves from time to time.  Then there is extended family.  You may not live with them but you still have to deal with them.  How many jokes have been told about Mother-In-Law's over the years?  The reason people find them funny is because they can often relate to them.

You'd think that getting away from the family would be an escape but then there is the boss, the co-workers, the neighbors, and even your friends.  Finally you have those that you don't necessarily know but you still have to interact with, like the cashier at the store, that person next to you on the road, the kid knocking on the door looking for a donation, or even the police woman that just pulled you over.  You simply can't get away from relationships.

Most people over the age of 30 have probably dreamed of living a solitary life at some point or another. Those dreams tend to revolve around a preferred getaway such as a tropical island, a beautiful home on the lake, a secluded place in the mountains, or a cabin out in the woods. We know deep down that we would hate living this way in short order, but it's kind of like winning the lottery. 'It may mess up everyone else's life but give me a shot...I think I can make it work.'

In reality, we need each other. We are created by God as social beings and without relationships in our lives most of us would go crazy. Few of us would even have the skills to survive on our own. While relationships can be broad and vary greatly, there are some Biblical principles that will strengthen almost any relationship imaginable. Apply these principles and watch your relationships improve...

**Love:** In the book of Matthew, a lawyer tested Jesus by asking Him what the greatest commandment was. The Old Testament has hundreds of commandments and there is a good chance that this lawyer felt he could trip Jesus up with his question. Jesus did not pick one of the Ten Commandments, which is where most people would likely go. Instead he went straight to the heart of our relationship with God...

*... Thou shalt love the Lord thy God with all thy heart, and with all thy soul, and with all thy mind. 38 This is*

*the first and great commandment.* – Matthew 22:37-38

But Jesus did not stop there. He answered the lawyer's question but then went on to tell him the second greatest commandment…

*And the second is like unto it, Thou shalt love thy neighbour as thyself.* - Matthew 22:39

The Bible does not tell us how the lawyer responded to Jesus' answer but he was most likely surprised, impressed, or pleased with it. From a Biblical perspective, you simply cannot sum up God's desire for us in any better way: Love God completely and love others as much as we love ourselves. Jesus even stated as much in His final comment to the lawyer that day…

*On these two commandments hang all the law and the prophets.* - Matthew 22:40

If you make a study of scripture, every commandment in the Bible is in some way connected with our love for God or others. Jesus tells us that if we love Him we are to keep his commandments (John 14:15). He also tells us that people will know that we are His disciples by our love for one another (John 13:35). Few people truly love God with all of their hearts and even fewer love others as themselves. The sad part is how few people are even trying. God has given us a seemingly impossible mission but through the power of the Holy Ghost we can succeed!

So what does this have to do with relationships? Absolutely everything! If you apply nothing else from this book to your life, start focusing on how to truly love. Love God! Love your parents. Love your spouse. Love your children. Love your roommate. Love your In-Laws, your boss, your employees, your neighbor, your friends and acquaintances. Love that person that gets on your nerves. The Bible tells you to even love your enemy! Prove your love by your actions.

So often we struggle in relationships because we aren't receiving what we want from others. If we work on truly loving everyone, our focus will turn from what we can get out of relationships to what we can give to them. True love destroys pride and cultures humility. It kills judgmental attitudes and awakens empathy. It tears down selfishness and builds up a selfless spirit. It weakens anger and strengthens patience.

Think about it. Pride, being judgmental, selfishness and anger are all personal traits that harm relationships. Humility, empathy, selflessness, and patience all strengthen relationships. How we view others in light of ourselves helps mold these character traits. Only when we learn to truly love will we reap the full benefits that we desire from our relationships! No matter how badly the other party may be treating you. No matter how hard you've tried to do the right thing. Ask yourself: Do I truly love them? Is it showing in my actions and my responses to them? We are almost always partly to blame in a poor relationship, or at the very least, we can respond in a more loving manner.

*Love is kind and patient, never jealous, boastful, proud, or rude. Love isn't selfish or quick tempered. It doesn't keep a record of wrongs that others do. Love rejoices in the truth, but not in evil. Love is always supportive, loyal, hopeful, and trusting. Love never fails!*
1 Corinthians 13:4-8 (CEV)

**The golden rule:** I've heard it said that every major religion has some form of the golden rule: 'Do unto others as you would have done unto you.' The Bible implies this throughout scripture and Jesus himself affirms it for us…

*Therefore all things whatsoever ye would that men should do to you, do ye even so to them: for this is the law and the prophets.* - Matthew 7:12

The golden rule is a principle that we will apply automatically if we love others but we need wisdom in properly understanding how to apply it. As a parent, I don't give a child everything they want just because I would like someone to give me everything I want. I don't give into that child just because they throw a fit. I don't withhold discipline from that child just because it will hurt them. As an adult I understand that constantly appeasing a child in the present is actually hurting that child's future. Just as I want to be a mature, responsible adult, it's my obligation as a parent to help my children become the same. Therefore I don't cater to their every whim and desire. I do my best to treat them the way I would want to be treated, even though it may be harder for both of us sometimes. Even though it may hurt sometimes. And if I do it correctly, someday they will likely appreciate it.

The same is true in our relationships with others. If we truly love someone we don't just cater to their selfish desires. We don't allow them to treat us like a doormat, walking all over us. That can be the easy way out but it doesn't help the relationship and it certainly doesn't help them. We need to do what's best for them. Sometimes we have to do the hard things. Things that may temporarily hurt us and hurt them. It may cost us time, energy, and money, but we do it because we love them and because it's best for them. And if we do it correctly…if we do it in love…we have the best chance of strengthening the relationship, and each other's character. Ask yourself: If the roles were reversed, how would I want them to treat me? Then do it.

**Trust:** One of the Ten Commandments basically says 'do not lie.' Strong relationships are built upon a foundation of trust, which comes from honesty, dependability, kindness, and humility. **Honesty** in that people can trust you to be truthful in all situations (Exodus 20:16). **Dependability** in that people can trust you to follow through on your promises and responsibilities (Proverbs 25:13). **Kindness** in that you will treat them as you yourself wish to be treated (Matthew 7:12). And **Humility** in that you admit your mistakes when you mess up, seek forgiveness from those you have hurt, and do your best to right the wrong (Matthew 5:23-24).

To be truthful in all situations proves to others that you are trustworthy. If you get pulled over by a police officer, and lie to her in front of your children, why would they believe you in a difficult situation with them? If you lie for your boss, how can your boss trust that you don't lie to him? Being truthful in all things is the key to building trust in all relationships.

People who are irresponsible or consistently break their promises will always struggle with relationships while those who are dependable are refreshing...

*A messenger you can trust is just as refreshing as cool water in summer.* - Proverbs 25:13 (CEV)

Kind people attract others. It's easy to trust someone who is considerate of those around them.

RECEIVE POWER

The opposite of kindness is mean, inconsiderate, selfish, harsh, cruel, and even hatred[9]. These traits build fear and drive people away.

Finally, nobody is attracted to pride and arrogance. Humility, like kindness, tends to have the thoughts and feelings of others in mind rather than self. Humble people are careful not to offend and when they do mess up, they are repentant and do their best to make amends.

Broken trust is difficult to restore but don't lose hope. Be patient and do your best to portray the character traits of this chapter to those you have hurt in the past. Hopefully in time they will see that you are seriously striving to be trustworthy and the relationship will heal.

**Practice Empathy:** People in a relationship will not always see eye to eye on a given subject or situation. How each party handles these disagreements is critical to the wellbeing of the relationship. It's easy to start having a judgmental attitude about the other person's opinions or actions. Jesus warns us against this type of thinking...

*Don't condemn others, and God won't condemn you. 2 God will be as hard on you as you are on others! He will treat you exactly as you treat them. 3 You can see the speck in your friend's eye, but you don't notice the log in your own eye. 4 How can you say, "My friend, let me take the speck out of your eye," when you don't see the log in your own eye? 5 You're nothing but show-offs! First, take the log out of your own eye. Then you can see how to take the speck out of your friend's eye.* - Matthew 7:1-5 (CEV)

There are a number of points that can be gleaned from this section of verses, all which will help you in relationships…

1. We are not called to condemn (judge) others. If we do, God will judge us in a similar fashion.
2. We all have issues in our lives, which may even be larger than the other person's faults. Focus on your own imperfections first and address them. This helps build humility. After doing that you may be surprised to see just how small the other person's problem is. You may even come to the realization that you were wrong and they were right.
3. Jesus is not calling us to be blind to issues. We are called to help one another. But this requires clear vision and a right attitude.

Throughout the gospels (The gospels are Matthew, Mark, Luke, and John, where we read stories about the life of Christ), we see Jesus showing compassion on people. The only time Jesus showed a judgmental spirit was when he confronted religious leaders who were hypocrites (Matthew 23:1-36) and those who intentionally desecrated the Lords house (Matthew 21:12-13). This does not give us the privilege to judge others. Jesus made that clear in Matthew 7, which we just went over. However, it does help set a precedent that we should address issues we have jurisdiction over (See 'Lead by Serving' below). Even then we are to do it with love and compassion.

One of the best tools to help you do this well is to intentionally practice empathy. As the common saying goes, put yourself in the other person's shoes. They are looking at the situation from a different perspective than you are. If you can better understand their point of view, if you can better understand why they feel the way they do, then you have a better chance of finding common ground and strengthening the relationship.

The ultimate example of empathy is Jesus himself. The people he came to save were the ones that had him crucified. Yet while hanging on the cross in agony he prayed *'Father, forgive them; for they know not what they do'* (Luke 23:34). Jesus had every right to be filled with anger and hatred towards those killing him. Instead he was focusing on how they didn't understand what they were doing. Most of the people thought they were doing the right thing, with no realization of how horribly wrong they were. Jesus loved them enough to see their point of view, despite the pain they were inflicting on him. What an amazing God that we serve!

**Forgive:** People are going to hurt you. Even people that love and care deeply for you will hurt you. Often this is done unintentionally but when it's intentional it hurts even more.

When someone hurts us, we are called to forgive them. Jesus tells us that if we do not forgive others that God will not forgive us (Matthew 6:14-15). We dare not take an unforgiving attitude lightly. Learn to forgive people that hurt you. If you are struggling with this see the chapter on 'Power over Bitterness.'

*And be ye kind one to another, tenderhearted, forgiving one another, even as God for Christ's sake hath forgiven you.* - Ephesians 4:32

**Respect Authority:** In Daniel chapter 3 we find an interesting story. King Nebuchadnezzar built an image of gold almost 100 feet high. He then commanded all of his officials to come to the dedication where they were required to bow down and worship it. It was made clear that anyone refusing to bow would be killed by being thrown into a fiery furnace.

Being followers of the one true God, three men named Shadrach, Meshach, and Abednego refused to bow down and worship Nebuchadnezzar's idol. They were brought before the king who confronted them and even offered to give them another chance.

Their response to him was…

*If it be so, our God whom we serve is able to deliver us from the burning fiery furnace, and he will deliver us out of thine hand, O king. 18 But if not, be it known unto thee, O king, that we will not serve thy gods, nor worship the golden image which thou hast set up.* – Daniel 3:17-18

The King was so angry at their refusal to obey him that he had the furnace heated up seven times hotter than normal and had them bound and thrown in. The furnace was so hot that the guards who threw them into the furnace were killed but God worked a miracle and saved Shadrach, Meshach, and Abednego. All the fire did was burn off their bonds. The King could see them walking around in the fire along with a 4th person who Nebuchadnezzar claimed to be like the Son of God. Astonished, the King called them out of the fire, commended them for trusting in their God, and made a decree against anyone who would speak against their God.

This story is one of the few places in the Bible where you see a follower of God rebelling against an authority figure in their life. These men were in bondage under an ungodly regime and yet to this point we see no signs of rebellion. They were faithful workers in his government. We can glean three key points from the lives of these three men…

1. We are only allowed to disobey leadership in our lives if they are requiring us to go against a higher authority; in this case God.

2. When disobedience is in order, we are to do it peacefully and respectfully. As Christians, we are not called to participate in riots, revolts, and other negative types of behavior. We need to be portray exemplary ethics and behavior in the midst of our refusal to obey.

3. There is a good chance that if we should disobey authority that we won't want to. These three men simply had to bow down to an image to save their lives. They likely struggled with the decision to stand for what was right. We tend to want to rebel for all the wrong reasons and want to obey when we know we shouldn't.

God tells us to…

*Obey them that have the rule over you, and submit yourselves: for they watch for your souls, as they that must give account, that they may do it with joy, and not with grief: for that is unprofitable for you.* - Hebrews13:17

And that…

*…rebellion is as the sin of witchcraft, and stubbornness is*

*as iniquity and idolatry...* - 1 Samuel 15:23

We are living in a dangerous era where distrust and rebellion against authority is becoming the norm. As Christians we are called to be the opposite. Jesus said...

*Ye have heard that it hath been said, An eye for an eye, and a tooth for a tooth: 39 But I say unto you, That ye resist not evil: but whosoever shall smite thee on thy right cheek, turn to him the other also. 40 And if any man will sue thee at the law, and take away thy coat, let him have thy cloke also. 41 And whosoever shall compel thee to go a mile, go with him twain. 42 Give to him that asketh thee, and from him that would borrow of thee turn not thou away. 43 Ye have heard that it hath been said, Thou shalt love thy neighbour, and hate thine enemy. 44 But I say unto you, Love your enemies, bless them that curse you, do good to them that hate you, and pray for them which despitefully use you, and persecute you;* - Matthew 5:38-44

God calls for us to love and reach out to our enemy in kindness. This holds true even if that enemy is an authority figure. The best thing you can do is respect the position, submit to their demands (provided those demands are not against a higher authority), and do it in love. This is the last thing most people would want to do. It is normal to want to lash out in rebellion and see the person put in their place. That is why we need the power of the

## POWER IN RELATIONSHIPS

Holy Ghost to help us do what is right.

An attitude of rebellion will often hurt you more than the authority figure. For example: Many people have been passed over on promotions, been demoted, or have even lost their job trying to get a bad boss fired. Even if the issue with the boss gets addressed, you often look bad in the process and get hurt in the long run.

Plus: Rebellion tends to breed disunity in an organization. Disunity creates uncertainty and chaos, making it difficult to accomplish anything positive. For example: The purpose of a police force is to protect and to serve. Due to a few bad employees, people are rebelling against the entire force. As a result, good officer's hands are tied, they are expected to place their own lives in even more danger, and many good officers get hurt or leave the force. In the end we are less safe and more criminals are on the street.

Finally: If you feel you have a right to rebel against authority when they are taking advantage of you, it's only a matter of time until you choose to rebel when you simply disagree with them. For example: A father refuses to allow his teenager to attend a party because he believes there is a good chance that underage drinking will be taking place. Her desire to go makes her feel that he is simply trying to hurt her when in reality he is trying to protect her. In her mind, she has a right to rebel and sneaks out to the party. Whether the father was right or not, she blatantly disobeyed the authority in her life who actually had her best interest in mind.

Over time, bad authority is usually addressed by a higher authority. It is not your place to rebel against it. God calls you to submit to them, with a right attitude, whether they are right or wrong. If you ever question whether you should do anything otherwise, talk to your pastor for Biblical wisdom and guidance.

Shadrach, Meshach, and Abednego knew their place in society and in the government. They fulfilled their role, faithfully submitting to an evil empire. It was not until they were required to break a higher law that they resisted authority, and then they did it peacefully and respectfully. As a result God was given the glory and the three young men were saved. Your best chance at redemption in a bad relationship with authority is to follow the example of these three men...

**Lead by Serving:** On the other hand, sooner or later you will likely be in a place of leadership, having others under your authority.

In John chapter 13, Jesus teaches us the proper attitude for a leader. After eating supper with his disciples, Jesus got a towel, a basin of water, and washed his disciple's feet. In today's society this seems like a strange thing to do but in the Bible days it was very common. People wore sandals on their feet and due to the dusty conditions their feet got dirty quickly. It was common to provide water for your guests to wash their feet when they came into your home. Sometimes a servant would wash the guests' feet for them or the host would choose to honor their guest by washing their feet.[10]

Foot washing was considered a servants job. Jesus, God in flesh, was humbling himself before his disciples to the level of a servant. Peter was so uncomfortable with this role reversal that he actually said...

*...Lord, dost thou wash my feet?...Thou shalt never wash my feet...* - John 13:6,8

But Jesus made it clear to Peter that he needed to receive this act of servanthood by his master. Some believe that this story goes beyond the obvious physical lesson about leadership and humility, and that it also has a spiritual purpose. Whether this is true or not, Jesus made it clear that he was teaching us a lesson on leadership...

*If I then, your Lord and Master, have washed your feet; ye also ought to wash one another's feet. 15 For I have given you an example, that ye should do as I have done to you. 16 Verily, verily, I say unto you, The servant is not greater than his lord; neither he that is sent greater than he that sent him.* - John 13:14-16

Having a position of leadership does not make you any greater than the people you lead. Who hasn't seen someone get a position and have it go to their head? They Lord over other people, take advantage of them, and use the position for their own personal gain. This certainly does not help build strong relationships.

A true leader doesn't glory in their position. They are humbled by the level of responsibility placed on their shoulders. They not only want to lead, but they want to lead well. A true leader is a servant to those he leads...

*...whosoever would become great among you shall be your minister; and whosoever would be first among you shall be your servant: even as the Son of man came not to be ministered unto, but to minister...* -
Matthew 20:26-28

Leaders are responsible for setting clear expectations and holding people accountable. But they also need to encourage, train, support, assist, acknowledge, and even do the work if necessary or appropriate. If a leader is not willing to do the same work that he expects his people to do, then he is not qualified to lead (this is not saying that he should do the work...it's saying that he should be willing to if necessary or appropriate). A leader also should inspire, treat people with respect and consideration, and care about their wellbeing.

It all comes back to loving one another and following the golden rule. Whether your position is as simple as heading up a weekend get together, to parenting your children, to running a multi-million dollar company, good leaders treat others in the way they would want to be treated themselves. Lead with a servant heart, being thoughtful, respectful, and considerate of others.

**Choose Relationships Wisely:** The best way to have strong relationships is to be careful who you choose to have relationships with in the first place. Obviously we cannot choose all of our relations. A family comes with parents, siblings, and relatives. A job comes with a boss and co-workers. School comes with teachers and fellow students. A home comes with neighbors. A church comes with all types of members. Everywhere we go, we come into contact with people that we may have a one-time connection with or that we may come to know over time. As a Christian, we should do our best to make a positive impact on everyone we come into contact with. We don't shun people simply because they believe, think, or act differently than us. We don't avoid someone because their personality may get on our nerves. Jesus was even ridiculed by the religious elites for spending time with people whom they felt should be avoided or shunned...

*And it came to pass, as Jesus sat at meat in the house, behold, many publicans and sinners came and sat down with him and his disciples. 11 And when the Pharisees saw it, they said unto his disciples, Why eateth your Master with publicans and sinners?* - Matthew 9:10-11

We are called to love everyone. We don't avoid them. We definitely don't shun them. We show them God's love. What we do need to be careful about though is how close we allow ourselves to become with others.

Acquaintances can easily turn into close relationships and close relationships can turn into committed relationships. Close and committed relationships with the wrong people can cause great turmoil in your life. The Bible teaches us to love everyone but to be closely connected to those that are like minded in our faith...

*Be ye not unequally yoked together with unbelievers: for what fellowship hath righteousness with unrighteousness? and what communion hath light with darkness?* - 2 Corinthians 6:14

It's only logical that people with opposite viewpoints, hobbies, interests and lifestyles will struggle more in a close relationship than those with similar traits. It's also obvious that those who treat others poorly are going to hurt you if you get too close. So don't haphazardly jump into deep relationships. Protect yourself by being aware, keeping your guard up, and only opening yourself to those who are a good fit for who you are and what you are trying to be.

But what if you are already in a bad relationship? A lot depends on you, how strong you are, the type of relationship, and your level of commitment to that person. There is no black and white answer. You still need to love them but at the same time you can't allow them to destroy you. Friendships that have grown toxic, that are hurting you more than you are helping them, should usually be cut off. There is nothing to gain by continuing the relationship. In a work situation you have to ask yourself, is this job important enough to stay? In a family situation, is it bad enough to alienate yourself from a loved one? In a marriage commitment, have they broken their marriage vows?

Seek Godly counsel before cutting off a relationship. Understand both yourself and the person you are struggling with. Are you cutting it off for selfish reasons or because it's the right thing to do in the given situation?

Seek Godly counsel if staying in a bad relationship. Find friends and mentors who can encourage and

## RECEIVE POWER

support you through the process, helping you make wise decisions and stay strong.

Many people feel trapped in a relationship and do not know how to get out. This is one reason it's so important to choose wisely up front. On the other hand, face your fears, seek wise counsel, trust God, and take appropriate action.

So how do you have power in your relationships?
- First: Receive the power of the Holy Ghost by following Acts 2:38
  (See 'How do I receive the power' chapter)
- Love God with all of your heart, soul, and mind
- Love others as much as you love yourself
- Treat others in a way that is best for them (Golden Rule)
- Build trust: Be Honest, Dependable, Kind, and Humble
- Practice empathy
- Forgive those that hurt you
- Respect and submit to authority
- Lead with a servant heart
- Choose your relationships wisely
- Seek wise, Godly counsel when struggling

You cannot control how others treat you, or how they will react to the way you treat them. However, treating them God's way gives you the greatest opportunity for success in the relationship. How

POWER IN RELATIONSHIPS

we view others defines how we treat them. Whether subordinates, peers, or those in authority, we need to love, honor, and respect one another. Be the positive example. Don't bring issues into the relationship. Live with integrity. And in all things, love.

# Power Over Bitterness

Colleen's life had never looked better. She and her live in boyfriend, Roy, had recently come into the church and been filled with the power of the Holy Ghost. Their new life in Christ was filled with joy and excitement. Their relationship was growing stronger as they pursued God together and soon they were married. They lived in a beautiful home that they had built together. Their business was improving as Roy started treating his employees and customers more ethically. She couldn't ask for more.

But Roy was struggling with an internal battle. He wanted to do right but he couldn't let go of the many negative influences in his life. It challenged his relationship with God, his wife, his friends, and his employees. Colleen and others helped encourage and support him but his negative desires were overcoming the positive ones. He continued taking one step forward and two steps back, slowly getting farther away from God's will for his life. Finally he walked away from everything and dove headlong back into a life of sin.

Colleen was filled with despair. The man she had built her life around, the one she had sacrificed for, the one she never stopped supporting and encouraging had left her, leaving her feeling worthless and undesirable. In addition to that, he left her with a large mortgage and business debts that without him were impossible to pay. She went from being blessed with having everything to having nothing but debt, creditors calling, angry customers and employees to deal with. Since Roy's credit was bad to start with, everything was in Colleen's name. Now her credit was shot as she attempted to liquidate their assets and pay off their debts. She was not even sure where she would live in the near future.

Colleen struggled with depression; filled with anger, resentment and bitterness towards the man who had turned her world upside down. She begged God for help but no restoration took place. She went to friends and spiritual leaders for counsel, but there wasn't much they could do other than provide wisdom and encouragement. It took years to work her way out of the financial mess she had been plunged into and even longer to find healing for the emotional scars that she received.

Throughout the process though, Colleen never lost her hope and trust in God. Although it was a struggle, she continued to follow wise counsel and God's leading. Rather than allow life's pain to drive her away from God, it brought her closer to Him. While in the eyes of worldly success, Colleen has yet to come close to where she once was in terms of materialistic blessings, those things are no longer important to her. From a spiritual standpoint she is stronger now than ever before.

---

People will hurt you. It's just a matter of time. Some will be intentional. Others will be unintentional. Either way it will hurt and sometimes it hurts badly. It's natural to feel pain when you have been hurt by others. It's natural to be angry and resentful and to desire that the wrong be made right. It's human nature to desire revenge, punishment, and retribution. But it's extremely important that we address this pain correctly to avoid becoming bitter.

Bitterness is like having a wound that isn't cared for and thus won't heal. Whether small or large, an uncared for wound is likely to get infected, and infections can become life threatening. I recently heard someone on the radio say that 'Bitterness is the poison we drink hoping the other person will die'[16]. Bitterness does not affect the perpetrator, it affects those harboring it. It's critical to address the wound in your life from a Godly perspective, before it destroys you...

When you are wounded by someone, the emotional scars can run deep. One of the first things you need to do is take it to the Lord in prayer. As noted earlier in this book, you cannot fix others, you can only change yourself. Use your wounds to drive you to a deeper relationship with God. Don't just seek healing, seek Him! Pursue a whole new level with God and the power of the Holy Ghost in your life. As you do, you will find emotional wounds become less painful. This is because our emotions tend to feed our fleshly, or sinful nature. The closer we get to God the more our emotional state takes on a Godly nature…

*This I say then, Walk in the Spirit, and ye shall not fulfil the lust of the flesh.* – Galatians 5:16

As you seek the Lord, pray that He helps you through this challenge. Ask God for comfort, wisdom, and the right attitude towards the one who hurt you.

Another key strategy towards conquering bitterness is empathy. Bitterness tends to be self-focus while empathy is considering the feelings of the other party. It's easy to ignore the thoughts and feelings of those that have committed the offense. I have seen relationships ruined when the offending party had pure motives or was even doing what was best for the other person. Yes, sometimes people hurt you out of completely selfish motives, but can we say that we have never done the same thing ourselves? Put yourself in their shoes. Do your best to understand their point of view - their feelings, desires, and struggles. Bitterness tends to stem from selfishness. Get your focus off of self. Earnestly pray for the person that offended you. As we learned in the relationships chapter, we are called to love everyone. Can you honestly say that you love the one who hurt you? Pray not only for them but that God will give you a love for them.

*But I say unto you, Love your enemies, bless them that curse you, do good to them that hate you, and pray for them which despitefully use you, and persecute you;* - Matthew 5:44

Once you have the right attitude towards the person that has hurt you (love and empathy), there is a Biblical process for dealing with the situation…

*Moreover if thy brother shall trespass against thee, go and tell him his fault between thee and him alone: if he shall hear thee, thou hast gained thy brother. 16 But if he will not hear thee, then take with thee one or two more, that in the mouth of two or three witnesses every word may be established. 17 And if he shall neglect to hear them, tell it unto the church: but if he neglect to hear the church, let him be unto thee as an heathen man and a publican.* - Matthew 18:15-17

Note the key statement in verse 15. The ultimate goal is to restore the relationship if possible (gained thy brother). The best way to do this is to follow these simple steps that Jesus gave us…

1. Share your hurt with the person who offended you. Don't hold it in and stew over it. One of the worst things you can do is keep it to yourself. When you do this, the open wound is festering with no treatment taking place. Share it with him and him alone. Avoid spreading it around by sharing it with others. Don't complain about him. Don't talk about him behind his back. Don't judge him (See James 4:11-12). It should not be your goal to humiliate or embarrass him. You don't mend a relationship by making the other person look bad. This doesn't mean that you should never seek spiritual counsel before approaching the person. Sometimes that is necessary to both work up the courage to approach the person and to do it well. Approaching the person can be a very difficult step but it's necessary for the healing process to start taking place. Work up the courage to confront them in a loving and considerate manner. Yes, it's hard, but do it.

2. If that doesn't work, then find a couple of key people who can help you confront him. It is preferable that these people were witnesses to the offense. If there were no witnesses, then you

should look for help from those that both of you have a mutual respect for. The goal is not to get a team of backers for your side. The goal is to find people that have wisdom in helping restore the relationship. In the process of trying to get help, you may find that the offense wasn't as harsh as you originally perceived. You'll have a hard time finding help if people feel that you are being petty or selfish. They may even tell you so. Be honest with yourself. Is the offense worth taking to the next level or is it better to just let it go? A small wound like a papercut can really hurt but if you care for the cut it heals in a short time and is forgotten. You don't change your attitude towards paper. You don't throw it out and buy a different brand. You just keep working with the paper you have as if nothing ever happened. Relationships can be the same way. Sometimes people really hurt you but it's really nothing more than a papercut. Be honest with yourself. Address the wound, tell the person that they hurt you, and get over it. You are strong enough to handle it through the power of the Holy Ghost and the other strategies in this chapter. (This analogy is in reference to the rare papercut like you would get in real life. There is a popular saying of 'death by 1000 papercuts.' Small, intentional wounds that add up cannot be ignored. Continue through the steps.)

3. If your offender still refuses to hear you via your peers then you are forced to take the issue to the authorities. If you both go to the same church then you need to take the issue to your pastor. If you work together, then you need to approach an appropriate leader in the company. If you do not have an organization in common, you have to consider approaching the law. Once again, you need to question whether the offense is hurtful enough that it warrants taking it to this level. Is it your own selfish desires wanting some type of retribution or is the wound that deep? Some people jump straight to this step, expecting the authorities to take care of the problem for them. Nobody likes a neighbor who calls the cops on them. That does not heal relationships, it hinders them. This is why in most cases this is the third step and not the first. You need to expect to be a part of this step. Don't approach a pastor, boss, cop, etc with your problem, expecting that they will run with it while you do nothing. Once again, their goal should be bringing the two of you together, not creating a greater divide. Be ready and willing to approach the offending party with the authority figure. Now that you have taken this third step, you need to be ready and willing to follow the authorities leading and guidance. Chances are it will not come out exactly like you hoped or planned. The more people you get involved in the situation as you proceed through

these steps, the more opportunities for it to get messy and convoluted, especially if you are skipping previous steps or expectations in the process. Don't allow the process of dealing with one hurt to turn into more wounds. You can easily become bitter with the very people who are trying to help you. Examine your heart, motives, & attitude. Escalate the issue appropriately. You may even have to escalate to another or higher authority, but be prepared to accept the end results.

4. If after the first three steps your offender refuses to repent of his actions then it is necessary to sever the relationship. In most cases, this should only be done at the recommendation of the authority figures in your life. While many may see this as a final 'goodbye and good riddance step', that is not the attitude to have. Even this should be done in hope that the person will come to realize the gravity of their actions and find a place of repentance. On the other hand if they will not, it's important to distance yourself for protection. In many cases, it's not even possible to completely avoid the person. Note that verse 17 states that we are to treat them as a 'heathen' or 'publican.' In other words, as Christians we are to treat them as sinners. We may have interaction with them, but we don't have close, personal relationships with them. We continue to love and reach out to them (as

appropriate in the given situation), hoping that they will find their way to God, but we keep the relationship at arm's length...

*Recompense to no man evil for evil. Provide things honest in the sight of all men. 18 If it be possible, as much as lieth in you, live peaceably with all men. 19 Dearly beloved, avenge not yourselves, but rather give place unto wrath: for it is written, Vengeance is mine; I will repay, saith the Lord. 20 Therefore if thine enemy hunger, feed him; if he thirst, give him drink: for in so doing thou shalt heap coals of fire on his head. 21 Be not overcome of evil, but overcome evil with good.* – Romans 12:17-21

Obviously not every situation will fit this Biblical plan perfectly and one must use wisdom in approaching the situation. For example: Someone who is being assaulted by another should never approach that person alone. Do not place yourself in a dangerous situation. Go straight to an appropriate authority figure for help. On the other hand, one shouldn't get a divorce just because the husband blew their savings on a new boat and refuses to sell it. The four step process is a general guideline that has the best chance of producing positive results.

But this is not the end. Jesus went on to discuss the most critical step, which is forgiveness. We lightly touched on forgiveness in the chapter on relationships but I would like to dig deeper into it here. The first thing that we must understand about forgiveness is that we are first forgiven and then forgivers: We have hurt God. We have hurt others. Often unintentionally but sometimes we've done it on purpose. You may have regretted your action but the damage is done. Imagine what relationships would be like if nobody was willing to forgive.

Think of a child or teenager. Throughout their younger years, children can be extremely selfish, cruel, and even an embarrassment to their parents. If it wasn't for a parents undying love and forgiveness, most children would be disowned before they became adults. God, our heavenly Father, is the same way. We have hurt him time and again with our selfish desires and antics and yet he continues to love and care for us. He is calling us to follow in his footsteps and forgive others. When we realize the depth of forgiveness that has been extended to us, it's much easier to pay it forward towards others.

In verse 21, the apostle Peter appears to have been struggling with someone who kept hurting him. He was trying to show the love of God towards the person by forgiving them but the problem was not going away. Looking for guidance, he brought his question to Jesus…

## POWER OVER BITTERNESS

*Then came Peter to him, and said, Lord, how oft shall my brother sin against me, and I forgive him? till seven times? 22 Jesus saith unto him, I say not unto thee, Until seven times: but, Until seventy times seven.* – Matthew 18:21

Jesus then went on to tell a story to those who were there that day...

*...the kingdom of heaven likened unto a certain king, which would take account of his servants. 24 And when he had begun to reckon, one was brought unto him, which owed him ten thousand talents. 25 But forasmuch as he had not to pay, his lord commanded him to be sold, and his wife, and children, and all that he had, and payment to be made. 26 The servant therefore fell down, and worshipped him, saying, Lord, have patience with me, and I will pay thee all. 27 Then the lord of that servant was moved with compassion, and loosed him, and forgave him the debt. 28 But the same servant went out, and found one of his fellowservants, which owed him an hundred pence: and he laid hands on him, and took him by the throat, saying, Pay me that thou owest. 29 And his fellowservant fell down at his feet, and besought him, saying, Have patience with me, and I will pay thee all. 30 And he would not: but went and cast him into prison, till he should pay the debt. 31 So when his fellowservants saw what was done, they were very sorry, and came and told unto their lord all that was done. 32 Then his lord, after that he had called him, said unto him, O thou wicked servant, I forgave thee all that debt, because thou desiredst me: 33 Shouldest not thou also*

*have had compassion on thy fellowservant, even as I had pity on thee? 34 And his lord was wroth, and delivered him to the tormentors, till he should pay all that was due unto him. 35 So likewise shall my heavenly Father do also unto you, if ye from your hearts forgive not every one his brother their trespasses.* - Matthew 18:23-35

We don't know the exact difference between 100 pence and ten thousand talents, but the Pulpit commentary estimates it at 1:1,250,000. In other words, if the fellow servant owed $100, the servant owed $125,000,000. What Jesus was showing us in this story is that we can never forgive others to the level that God has forgiven us. Even if someone hurts us time and again, in the same exact way, how many times have we done the same toward God? Who are we to expect God to extend mercy towards us if we won't extend mercy towards others? He won't...

*For if ye forgive men their trespasses, your heavenly Father will also forgive you: 15 But if ye forgive not men their trespasses, neither will your Father forgive your trespasses.* - Matthew 6:14-15

So how do you have power over bitterness?
- First: Receive the power of the Holy Ghost by following Acts 2:38
  (See 'How do I receive the power' chapter)
- Understand that bitterness is self-destructive
- Earnestly seek God and his help through prayer

- Examine your own heart and motives. Do you need to change?
- Practice love and empathy towards your offender. Pray for them.
- Address the issue with the offender
- Attempt to restore the relationship while at the same trying to save face for the offender
- Escalate as appropriate and necessary until repentance takes place or you reach an impasse.
- If at an impasse, sever the relationship appropriately.
- Forgive

In the beginning of the chapter that we have been reviewing, the disciples asked Jesus who would be the greatest in the kingdom of heaven. His response was...

*...Jesus called a little child unto him, and set him in the midst of them, 3 And said, Verily I say unto you, Except ye be converted, and become as little children, ye shall not enter into the kingdom of heaven. 4 Whosoever therefore shall humble himself as this little child, the same is greatest in the kingdom of heaven.* – Matthew 18:2-4

Jesus specifically stated that being humble, like a small child, was not only what makes you great in the kingdom of heaven, but that it's required to even get in. I believe the rest of the chapter reveals the depth of humility that God is calling us to. As followers of Christ, we are not called to damage relationships but to build them. We have no right to retaliate, have a judgmental attitude, be bitter, or refuse forgiveness to those who have hurt us. I once heard someone say that 'bitterness is always against God.' Bitterness in and of itself is the act of withholding forgiveness and when we choose not to forgive, we are placing ourselves in a higher position than God himself. Therefore, our bitterness truly is an offense against God.

One beautiful aspect of small children is their inability to hold a grudge. They don't keep score. They don't nurse offenses. They are quick to forgive. Quick to love. They are beautiful in their youthful innocence and humility. God is calling you to be the same.

*Let all bitterness, and wrath, and anger, and clamour, and evil speaking, be put away from you, with all malice: 32 And be ye kind one to another, tenderhearted, forgiving one another, even as God for Christ's sake hath forgiven you.* - Ephesians 4:31-32

# Power At Your Job

*Choose a job you love, and you will never have to work a day in your life.* – Author Unknown[14]

The above quote is such a profound statement, and should be taken seriously by all who are considering a career choice, but few are blessed to find this path in their lives. At the very least, we should pursue a job that we find interesting, but even that is not always possible.

I like my job, I like the people I work with, and I enjoy being at work. I am both blessed with and thankful for my job. But there are also tasks and expectations of my job that I don't like. I do not look forward to getting up early each morning to go and there are certainly things that I would rather be doing. As much as I enjoy my job, the only reason I go is because of the pay. When I hear people complaining about their job, I like to say 'That is why they call it a job. If it was something you wanted to do, they wouldn't be paying you to do it.'

For this very reason, too many people approach their jobs with the wrong attitude to start with.

They don't want to be there, they may not even like being there, the people they work with may be difficult, but they need the money. It's easy to develop a bad attitude about your job, which in turn affects the quality and quantity of your work, which ends up creating further issues, making you like your job even less. In a way it can become a self-fulfilling prophecy.

Understand that it is possible to scrub toilets, dig ditches, and do any other menial or labor intensive task and actually enjoy your work. The Bible gives us a few key guidelines that relate to having power at our job...

To start with, understand that the joy of the Lord is our strength (Nehemiah 8:10) which we gain through the power of the Holy Ghost...

*Now the God of hope fill you with all joy and peace in believing, that ye may abound in hope, through the power of the Holy Ghost.* - Romans 15:13

When we are filled with the joy of the Lord, having a song in our hearts, it's easy to work through undesirable circumstances. Stop focusing on the negative task in front of you and start focusing on the goodness of the Lord. Allow your heart to be lifted up in a spirit of praise, worship, and thanksgiving and see how fast the day goes by.

## POWER AT YOUR JOB

Secondly: Studies have shown that when you can find purpose in your work that you can find fulfilment in it. I believe the Lord gave us the following verse partially for this reason…

*And whatsoever ye do, do it heartily, as to the Lord, and not unto men;* - Colossians 3:23

Some people can find fulfilment in their work because they are an integral part of saving or improving the lives of others. But let's face it: When it comes right down to it, many of us are employed in areas where we are nothing more than a cog in a wheel, helping make the people above us more money than we make ourselves. If we view our jobs this way, it's hard not to have a complacent attitude about our work. The Lord says not to view our jobs this way. Look at the task that you are assigned to do as if the Lord himself asked you to do it, and dive into that task whole heartedly. Work hard and take pride in your work. As stated in one of Martin Luther King Junior's speeches, do your job so well that the hosts of heaven and earth take notice…

*If a man is called to be a streetsweeper, he should sweep streets even as Michelangelo painted, or Beethoven played music, or Shakespeare wrote poetry. He should sweep streets so well that all the hosts of heaven and earth will pause to say, here lived a great streetsweeper who did his job well.* - Martin Luther King, Jr [15]

## RECEIVE POWER

The quality and quantity of our work is a direct reflection of the God we serve. People who claim to be Christians that are poor employees give both Christianity and God a bad name. Let your labor be a testimony to the greatness of God in your life.

If we are truly doing our work as unto the Lord, then we will be doing our best whether others are looking or not. We will be a good employee whether management notices or not. We will work hard because that is both our employer's and our Lord's expectation…

*Servants, be obedient to them that are your masters according to the flesh, with fear and trembling, in singleness of your heart, as unto Christ; Not with eyeservice, as menpleasers; but as the servants of Christ, doing the will of God from the heart; With good will doing service, as to the Lord, and not to men: -* Ephesians 6:5-7 (Also see Colossians 3:22)

Even if management doesn't seem to notice or care, you can rest assured that God does. Train yourself to always work as if the owner were standing behind you watching, because even if she isn't, the Lord is.

Finally: Be content with your benefit package…

*And the soldiers likewise demanded of him, saying, And what shall we do? And he said unto them, Do violence to* *no man, neither accuse any falsely; and <u>be content with your wages</u>.* - Luke 3:14

I've worked with a number of people that had nothing good to say about the company they worked for. Some have left, only to try returning after trying other jobs. The grass always looks greener on the other side of the fence but once you climb over you find that it often isn't. Rather than focusing on what your job isn't giving you, focus on what it is. Rather than focusing on others that have it better, focus on those that have it worse. Once your perspective is in the right place, if you still cannot be content in the position that you have, then it's your responsibility to leave. If you truly believe you deserve more than what you are currently making, then it's up to you to go find it. Discontent employees do not reach their full potential. To stay in your current state of discontent is cheating both your company and yourself.

One thing we did not cover in this chapter is employee/employer relationships because it's mostly addressed in the Power in Relationships chapter. The relational advice that God gives us in the Bible is as true in the workplace as anywhere else. It's important that we respect and obey management, lead humbly with a servant spirit, and love all. If you are having any challenges with relationships at work then I strongly recommend reading the Power in Relationships chapter.

RECEIVE POWER

So how do you have power at your job?
- First: Receive the power of the Holy Ghost by following Acts 2:38
  (See 'How do I receive the power' chapter)
- Have a proper attitude towards and treat others appropriately, whether authority, peers, or subordinates (Power in Relationships chapter)
- Work hard, doing it for the Lord, whether people are watching or not
- Be content with your position or find another job
- Pursue the joy of the Lord as you work

When I was young, the economy went through a recession and my father was laid off from his job. While looking for work that paid enough to support his family, he took a position at the county garage as a non-skilled laborer for a short time. Years later our church was constructing a new building. We needed a culvert for the new driveway and dad recommended we check with the county garage, knowing they stocked various sizes. Our pastor went over to check into it and mentioned that he knew Tom Saburn who had once worked there. The man helping our pastor told him that nobody had ever worked as hard as Tom did for the low wage that they paid.

People are watching you work. Are you doing it as unto the Lord?

# Power In Your Finances

*A land owner once planted a vineyard. He built a wall around it and dug a pit to crush the grapes in. He also built a lookout tower. Then he rented out his vineyard and left the country. When it was harvest time, the owner sent some servants to get his share of the grapes. But the renters grabbed those servants. They beat up one, killed one, and stoned one of them to death. He then sent more servants than he did the first time. But the renters treated them in the same way. Finally, the owner sent his own son to the renters, because he thought they would respect him. But when they saw the man's son, they said, "Someday he will own the vineyard. Let's kill him! Then we can have it all for ourselves." So they grabbed him, threw him out of the vineyard, and killed him. Jesus asked, "When the owner of that vineyard comes, what do you suppose he will do to those renters?" The chief priests and leaders answered, "He will kill them in some horrible way. Then he will rent out his vineyard to people who will give him his share of grapes at harvest time."* - Matthew 21:33-41 (CEV)

The Bible talks about money more than any other subject and well it should. Being the main form of exchange throughout history, money is an important tool in each of our lives. As a result it is very easy for us to develop a non-Biblical viewpoint on money and over time money can hurt us more than help. One of the top issues in marriages today is finances. It could be argued that excessive debt and bankruptcies are hitting epidemic levels in society. Entire corporations fail due to greed and corruption. Those that have plenty of money are often discontent and want even more.

The Bible tells us in 1 Timothy 6:10 that *'the love of money is the root of all evil.'* While we are never called to hate money, it is important that we have the proper attitude towards it. If we handle our finances in a Godly manner, our lives will be blessed. No matter how entrenched we are, whether it be excessive debt or the pursuit of riches, the power of the Holy Ghost and Biblical insights can help you overcome your financial struggles.

The first thing we must understand is that we are not the source of our financial empire, God is. He created everything and He owns everything...

*The earth is the LORD's, and the fulness thereof; the world, and they that dwell therein. 2 For he hath founded it upon the seas, and established it upon the floods.* - Psalms 24:1-2

*For every beast of the forest is mine, and the cattle upon a thousand hills. 11 I know all the fowls of the mountains: and the wild beasts of the field are mine 12 ...for the world is mine, and the fulness thereof.* - Psalms 50:10-12

I'm reminded of a story I heard years ago that went something like this: A pastor went out to visit one of his parishioners who was a successful farmer. The farmer gave him a tour of his many fields and everywhere they went the pastor would exclaim "Wow! God has really blessed you." The farmer grew more and more irritated with this response until he finally said "Reverend, you should have seen these fields when just God had them."

You may have spent years of hard work accumulating the wealth and financial status you have today. God made it clear in the beginning that we would have to toil for what we get out of life (Genesis 3:17-19) and those efforts are commendable. However, it is important to understand that there are people who are smarter and have worked harder than you who have failed. There are also people who are more successful who have not put in near the effort. The Bible tells us…

*I returned, and saw under the sun, that the race is not to the swift, nor the battle to the strong, neither yet bread to the wise, nor yet riches to men of understanding, nor yet favour to men of skill; but time and chance happeneth to them all.* – Ecclesiastes 9:11

What we must understand about money is that the amount we have is not what's important but rather our attitude towards it and how we use it. Every dollar we have is a blessing from God and how we use it defines us. God has entrusted us with some of His wealth and expects us to use it wisely. This is referred to as stewardship: We do not own our money but rather we manage it for the Lord.

If we truly understand that God is the owner of all things, and if we truly love Him more than anything else (as noted in the relationships chapter), then we will have a natural desire to give back to God some of the blessing that he has entrusted us with. Putting God first in our money is a critical first step to having power over our finances. This is commonly known as the concept of first fruits: The very first thing that we take out of our income is that which we give back to God. So what does the Bible teach us to give back to Him? Tithe and offering…

*Will a man rob God? Yet ye have robbed me. But ye say, Wherein have we robbed thee? In tithes and offerings.* - Malachi 3:8

When we do not support God's kingdom by giving back to it with our tithes and offerings we are actually robbing from God. Many people contend that tithing is an Old Testament concept that is no longer required of us today but there is simply no Biblical support for this viewpoint. In fact, Jesus himself claims we ought to tithe even on small things that may seem insignificant…

*But woe unto you, Pharisees! for ye tithe mint and rue and all manner of herbs, and pass over judgment and the love of God: these ought ye to have done, and not to leave the other undone.* - Luke 11:42

So what is tithe? By definition it is a tenth of your income. While we won't go into detail here, the tithe is designed to support the ministry and should go directly to your local church. In our opening story, you could look at the rent required by the landowner as tithing. We do not have any control over what our tithe is used for or the amount to give. When we tithe, we are simply returning to God what He is due. This is often referred to as God's portion of our income and He chooses how it is spent.

So what is offering and how is it different than tithing? Offering is what we choose to give above and beyond our tithe. In our opening story, the renters may have invested some of their own funds back into the vineyard to help improve or maintain it. This would be similar to an offering. People tend to invest in causes that they believe in. The amount we give is our choice and many choose to give to specific needs…

*Every man according as he purposeth in his heart, so let him give; not grudgingly, or of necessity: for God loveth a cheerful giver.* – 2 Corinthians 9:7

While tithe is intended to support the ministry of the church, our offerings support the remaining financial needs. Without both, the church cannot function as God intends. Our sacrificial giving to the kingdom of God is a key component to a healthy church.

At this point you may be feeling that this is compounding your financial woes rather than helping them. It's important to understand that if you have the right Biblical foundation and attitude towards money, you can control it rather than have your finances control you. This starts with putting God first in your life financially.

The second critical element of financial freedom is contentment. Our opening story does not share how steep the rent on the vineyard was, but it implies that the renters had a good thing going. Rather than being thankful for what they had, their desire for more drove them to their own destruction. This is a very typical illustration of an affluent society. It is important to understand that materialistic things do not bring happiness. True peace, joy, and contentment only comes from God. This is why Jesus told us to…

*Lay not up for yourselves treasures upon earth, where moth and rust doth corrupt, and where thieves break through and steal: 20 But lay up for yourselves treasures in heaven, where neither moth nor rust doth corrupt, and where thieves do not break through nor steal: 21 For where your treasure is, there will your heart be also.* - Matthew 6:19-21

The closer we are to God, the easier it is to be content with the basic necessities of life. The more we get caught up in the things of this world the more distant we will be from God, the less content we will be with what we have, and the more challenges we will bring upon ourselves…

*But godliness with contentment is great gain. 7 For we brought nothing into this world, and it is certain we can carry nothing out. 8 And having food and raiment let us be therewith content. 9 But they that will be rich fall into temptation and a snare, and into many foolish and hurtful lusts, which drown men in destruction and perdition. 10 For the love of money is the root of all evil: which while some coveted after, they have erred from the faith, and pierced themselves through with many sorrows.* – 1 Timothy 6:6-10

Understand that there is nothing wrong with having things. God is not calling us to a life of poverty and basic subsistence. What he is calling us to is putting him first, enjoying his blessings, but not getting caught up in those blessings. If something is starting to control us, the best thing we can do is get rid of it…

*Wherefore seeing we also are compassed about with so great a cloud of witnesses, let us <u>lay aside every weight, and the sin which doth so easily beset us</u>, and let us run with patience the race that is set before us, 2 Looking unto Jesus the author and finisher of our faith; who for the joy that was set before him endured the cross, despising the shame, and is set down at the right hand of the throne of God.* - Hebrews 12:1-2

So what God is basically calling us to do is to live within our means. When we put God first, and learn to be content with what we have, then living within our means is quite doable for most people. Being a good steward of the money God has blessed us with means we control our impulsive desires and only purchase what we can afford. It means we don't spend every dollar we make but we are actually able to save for unexpected expenses and to help others in need…

*Give to him that asketh thee, and from him that would borrow of thee turn not thou away.* - Matthew 5:42

It means we avoid debt as much as possible…

*The rich ruleth over the poor, and the borrower is servant to the lender.* - Proverbs 22:7

Society is starting to pick up on the freedom found in minimalism. We don't own things, they tend to own us. The less we have, the more time and finances we have available for ourselves, God, and others.

So how do you have power in your finances?
- First: Receive the power of the Holy Ghost by following Acts 2:38
(See 'How do I receive the power' chapter)
- Understand that everything you have is entrusted to you by God
- Put God first in your finances, paying your tithe and giving offerings
- Be thankful for and content with what God has blessed you with
- Live within your means
- Avoid unnecessary debt
- Build up savings for unexpected expenses and to help others

For those who are currently in over their heads, it's critical that you commit yourself to fixing your financial crisis. Not only do you need to follow the previous points, but you need to live well below your means until you are caught back up. This may require cutting expenses, selling assets, consolidating debt, and even taking on additional work. Your situation may seem impossible on the surface but there is hope. Many have been in your situation and have overcome it.

Your first and most important step is to put God

first. However, you cannot do this by ignoring your bills. As a Christian, you are responsible for paying your debts (Psalms 37:21, Romans 13:7-8). You need to figure out where to cut expenses or offset your income. When you put God first he promises to protect you from unexpected expenses that tend to 'devour' your income...

*Bring ye all the tithes into the storehouse, that there may be meat in mine house, and <u>prove me now</u> herewith, saith the LORD of hosts, if I will not open you the windows of heaven, and pour you out a blessing, that there shall not be room enough to receive it. 11 And <u>I will rebuke the devourer</u> for your sakes, and <u>he shall not destroy the fruits of your ground</u>; neither shall your vine cast her fruit before the time in the field, saith the LORD of hosts.* - Malachi 3:10-11

Put God first, trust in Him, and commit yourself to having power over your finances.

# Power to Persevere

The power of the Holy Ghost can accomplish amazing things in your life but God did not bless you with this precious gift for selfish gain. Some people serve God under the false pretense that they will receive everything their heart desires. This ideal is not found in the Bible and can actually be quite destructive...

*The heart is deceitful above all things, and desperately wicked: who can know it?* – Jeremiah 17:9

God is our heavenly father. Just as a wise parent protects their small child from a hot stove, God protects us from things that will burn us. Fame, fortune, power, and other seemingly positive things have destroyed many people. If God simply blessed us with all of our hearts desires, whether good or bad, chances are they would hurt us more than help. Even Solomon, the wisest man to ever live (1 Kings 3:12), misused the blessings of God to his own hurt.

Christians are no different than non-Christians in a lot of respects: They get sick, face financial hardships, tragedies, and even premature death. The Bible tells us that *'he maketh his sun to rise on the evil and on the good, and sendeth rain on the just and on the unjust.'* (Matthew 5:45) and that *'time and chance happeneth to them all'* (Ecclesiastes 9:11). Good things happen to bad people and bad things happen to good people

While we avoid many hardships in life by living a sin free lifestyle, we are likely to face other types of challenges because of our commitment to God. The Bible tells us that we may be hated for following Jesus (Matthew 10:22, 24:9); That we may be persecuted (Matthew 10:23, 24:9); That our own family may turn against us (Matthew 10:21); and that we may even be called to die for our faith (Hebrews 11). You are very likely to face negative things in your life as a result of your commitment to God.

God did not promise to bless us with all of our fleshly desires. He also did not promise to protect us from hardship. As much as we may wish it were otherwise, serving God is not a free pass from the toils of life. Our heavenly father understands that trials create better and stronger individuals. What he does give us is better...

**Protection**
*There hath no temptation taken you but such as is common to man: but God is faithful, who will not suffer*

*you to be tempted above that ye are able; but will with the temptation also make a way to escape, that ye may be able to bear it.* – 1 Corinthians 10:13

While Christians face the same types of challenges that non-Christians face, God has promised us that He will not allow anything in our life that we cannot handle. No matter how dark life may seem, God is with us and will see us through it. This is not promised to non-Christians.

### Positive Results
*And we know that all things work together for good to them that love God, to them who are the called according to his purpose.* – Romans 8:28

This is a popular verse for people going through difficulties. What is often missed or ignored is that this promise is only for those who love God and are following after Him. When we have the Holy Ghost in our lives, we can know that God is working through our difficulties to reap positive results.

### Contentment
*Not that I speak in respect of want: for I have learned, in whatsoever state I am, therewith to be content. 12 I know both how to be abased, and I know how to abound: every where and in all things I am instructed both to be full and to be hungry, both to abound and to suffer need. 13 I can do all things through Christ which strengtheneth me.* - Philippians 4:11-13

Have you ever watched small children playing in the same room? A child can be perfectly content playing with a toy, but when they see another child having fun with something else, they will drop everything and immediately want what the other child has. Sad to say, adults are not much different. They just aren't as obvious. What was so important at one point in life gets replaced by the desire for something new and different. Without God, contentment is a never ending quest. There is a reason that personal debt is becoming an epidemic. Humanity is pursuing contentment through temporal things which will never work. With the Holy Ghost in our lives, we can learn to be content in whatever state we find ourselves, whether good or bad.

**Joy, Peace, and Hope**
*Now the God of hope fill you with all joy and peace in believing, that ye may abound in hope, through the power of the Holy Ghost.* - Romans 15:13

Not only can we be content in our situation, but we can have peace throughout our struggles, knowing that God is with us and will see us through. We can have joy in our circumstances, knowing that life's problems are not what define us. We can have hope throughout our lives, knowing that God is working good through it. In light of eternity with God in heaven, our temporary struggles will eventually seem minor and insignificant.

The Holy Ghost gives us power to persevere! No matter what the situation in life, we can have the right spirit and attitude as we progress through it…

*I can do all things through Christ which strengtheneth me.* - Philippians 4:11-13

We can use our circumstances to turn our backs on God, or we can use them to turn ourselves towards Him even more. God is looking for total trust and commitment, not for selfish, fair weather friends…

*…he that endureth to the end shall be saved* - Matthew10:22, 24:13, Mark 13:13

So build a strong relationship with the Lord! Be filled with the power of the Holy Ghost. Spend time daily with God in prayer and Bible reading. Become an integral part of his family by joining a church that preaches full Bible truth, including Acts 2:38. Pursue a sin free lifestyle that is pleasing to Him, having a repentant heart when you make a mistake. Follow the wisdom found in God's word and then, no matter what may take place in your life, trust in God's promises whole heartedly and allow Him to answer on His time…

RECEIVE POWER

*Trust in the LORD with all thine heart; and lean not unto thine own understanding.*
Proverbs 3:5

*But they that wait upon the LORD shall renew their strength; they shall mount up with wings as eagles; they shall run, and not be weary; and they shall walk, and not faint.*
Isaiah 40:31

# Summary

God has given us themes throughout the Bible to live an overcoming and abundant life. Live a healthier and happier life by seeking God, studying His Word, and applying it. Many of these themes have been woven into this book.

Some are themes of understanding, such as…
- You were made by God, in His image, and God does not make mistakes
- While you may have worked hard for them, every material thing you have attained in this life is a blessing from the Lord
- You can grow through suffering hardships and God can receive glory in the process
- In light of eternity with God, our suffering on earth is a wisp in time
- All things work together for good to those that love the Lord
- God will always be there for you, even if it doesn't feel like He is
- God has forgiven our insurmountable debt of sin
- The joy of the Lord is our strength

While others are themes of action…
- Trust in the Lord with all of your heart. Give your cares and worries to Him.
- Be thankful for and content with what you have rather than focus on what you don't have
- Allow hardships to turn you towards God rather than away
- Love God with all of your heart, and others as yourself
- Focus outward rather than on yourself. Make a difference for God and in the lives of others
- Put God first in your life, letting it show through how you use your time, talents, and finances
- Confess your faults and get the help you need
- Seek reconciliation when you offend others
- Address issues rather than allow them to grow
- Be quick to forgive
- Continually pursue a closer relationship with God
- Remove sources of temptation from your life
- Do your work heartily, as if you were doing it directly for the Lord
- Keep a positive attitude and never give up
- Give God the glory in everything that you do

Entire books have been written on each of these subjects. While this book is by no means exhaustive, if you honestly apply these principles to your life you will see the power of the Holy Ghost work positive change. Don't stop there though. Continue to learn and grow.

Having the power of God in your life by receiving the Holy Ghost will give you the strength and ability to apply these strategies, but we can't do it alone. We need each other to train, encourage, and motivate us. Find a mentor and friend. Find someone filled with the Holy Ghost that is on fire for the Lord and grow with them. Find someone that will teach you a home Bible study. Find someone that is ahead of you in their pursuit of God and follow their example.

We will never reach perfection. We will always be challenged and struggle with certain traits in our lives. But through the power of the Holy Ghost, a daily relationship with God, and the support of one another we can grow stronger each day. Start now and see what God can do in your life!

***If you are guided by the Spirit, you won't obey your selfish desires***. 17 The Spirit and your desires are enemies of each other. They are always fighting each other and keeping you from doing what you feel you should. 18 But if you **obey the Spirit**, the Law of Moses has no control over you. 19 People's desires make them give in to immoral ways, filthy thoughts, and shameful deeds. 20 They worship idols, practice witchcraft, hate others, and are hard to get along with. People become jealous, angry, and selfish. They not only argue and cause trouble, but they are 21 envious. They get drunk, carry on at wild parties, and do other evil things as well. I told you before, and I am telling you again: No one who does these things will share in the blessings of God's kingdom. 22 God's Spirit makes us loving, happy, peaceful, patient, kind, good, faithful, 23 gentle, and self-controlled. There is no law against behaving in any of these ways. 24 And **because we belong to Christ Jesus, we have killed our selfish feelings and desires**.

Galatians 5:16-24 (CEV)

# References

Most of the stories in this book are either true or based on actual events. Names and details have been changed for those who prefer to remain anonymous.

[1] Strong's Hebrew and Greek Dictionaries
[2] Webster's 1828 Dictionary
[3] Pulpit Commentary
[4] Matthew Henry Commentary
[5] Wikipedia.org
[6] https://www.psychologytoday.com/us/basics/anxiety
[7] https://www.psychologytoday.com/us/basics/depression
https://www.psychologytoday.com/us/conditions/depressive-disorders
[8] https://en.wikipedia.org/wiki/Footprints_(poem)
[9] www.thesaurus.com
[10] Wycliffe Bible Encyclopedia
[11] https://www.verywellmind.com/overcoming-addiction-4157285
[12] https://www.biblegateway.com
[13] https://en.wikipedia.org/wiki/This_too_shall_pass
[14] https://quoteinvestigator.com/2014/09/02/job-love/
[15] https://www.passiton.com/inspirational-quotes/3684-if-a-man-is-called-to-be-a-

streetsweeper-he - It appears that MLK Jr. gave this speech more than once with variations in the text

[16] Variations of this statement have been credited to many but quoteinvestigator.com credits the original to "The Angry Christian" by Bert Ghezzi - https://quoteinvestigator.com/2017/08/19/resentment/

[17] Some believe that there were 10 days between Jesus' ascension and the day of Pentecost while others contend that it was only 7 days

[18] Raised From The Dead Article, The Pentecostal Herald Magazine, 2005 Special Issue, United Pentecostal Church International

[19] Get with the program | God's Program | A Christian perspective of Alcoholism and Drug Addiction by Cynthia T. Adams, Insignia Publications

Made in United States
Orlando, FL
29 March 2022